THE
CHICKEN
THAT
WON A
DOGFIGHT

"Such wit!"

—William V. Driscoll
American Paper Institute
New York, NY

"Ben Burton draws one into his web of joy."

—Edward L. Williams
Winrock International
Morrilton, AR

*"Reading Ben Burton on the plane shortens the trip
and lightens the load."*

—Jeanne Robertson, CSP, CPAE

THE CHICKEN THAT WON A DOGFIGHT

BEN BURTON

August House Publishers, Inc.
LITTLE ROCK

Published by August House, Inc.,
P.O. Box 3223, Little Rock, Arkansas, 72203,
501-372-5450

Printed in the United States of America

10 9 8 7 6 5 4 3 2 1

LIBRARY OF CONGRESS CATALOGING IN PUBLICATION DATA
Burton, Ben, 1929-
The chicken that won a dogfight: the humor and hope of an Arkansas
boyhood / Ben Burton : with Foreword by Bill Clinton
P. cm.
ISBN 0-87483-259-4 (hb: alk. paper)
ISBN 0-87483-258-8 (pb: alk. paper)
1. Arkansas—Social life and customs, humor
2. Burton, Ben, 1029—Childhood and youth, humor
I. Title
F411.6.C48   1992
976.7'052'0207—dc20   92-35636 CIP

Executive: Ted Parkhurst
Editor: Lou Ann Norman
Cover design: Harvill-Ross Studios Ltd.
Text illustration: Jon Kennedy
Typography: Heritage/North Little Rock

This book is printed on archival-quality paper which meets the guidelines for performance and durability of the Committee on Production
Guidelines for Book Longevity of the Council on Library Resources.

AUGUST HOUSE, INC.   PUBLISHERS   LITTLE ROCK

Dedication

*To LaVerne, who provides that best light
in which she has always seen me
and without whom there would be no book
and little joy.*

Contents

Foreword

Ben Burton causes people to laugh—with him, and at
him, and at themselves and each other. He does it as well
and as often as anyone I know in Arkansas.

It hasn't always been so.

When Ben Burton came to Hot Springs High School to
coach football my senior year there, if he was funny, he
was the only one who knew it. We students never would
have guessed it.

We did learn this about Ben: he was and is a gentle and
sensitive person who cared deeply about people. He hurt
for us and with us when we failed to meet our goals.

Ben Burton's roots are in Southwest Arkansas, only
forty miles from mine at Hope, where there was a good
measure of hurt but never a shortage of laughter or hope.

Students of humor and our own observations teach us
that humor and pathos are often closely coupled. This is
true in Burton's life and in his writing.

In the stories that follow, Ben Burton recalls with
refreshing originality and humor the ingenuousness of a
late depression-day childhood in a section of our country
where, then and now, families are close, values are firm,
and hope endures.

I promise the sensitive reader an absence of despair, a
lot of laughs, and even a tear of joy or two.

Bill Clinton
President of the United States

Introduction

This is the book I began fifty-six years ago. Well, not exactly.

As a poor, timid, six-year-old south Arkansas farm boy, hollow with a non-specific sorrow while brimming with a boundless joy, I wrote my first book, *Poverty Can Be Paradise*.

Actually I only got as far as the title. But I never got over that *Poverty Can Be Paradise* feeling. The feeling then (and now) was this: "I cannot leave all those people out there—you and the others—burdened with the idea that our plight is as dismal as it appears."

I wanted you and the others to know how much fun we were having—to let you all know how good life was from our side of the road. I wanted to acquit Mother and Dad, should anyone blame them. (What's to blame?) I hoped to show you our pain, but for only one purpose, to have you laugh, recover, and rejoice with us.

Those feelings were strong. However I never wrote one word of *Poverty Can Be Paradise*.

Long after I started telling and writing some of these old stories and a book began to germinate, an emerging thesis occurred to me that was a familiar one. I was writing the book I *saw and felt* as a child.

Please! Not for a moment do I allot any virtue to poverty. Absolutely not. Neither, however, do I equate impoverishment—of the kind we experienced—with unhappiness and hopelessness.

So I offer you these tales of blissful ignorance, not to have you grieve, but to have you join us, to laugh at us and with us, and to lighten your load.

The common thread you'll find woven through most of these country awakenings of the twin Burtons is *ignorance*, or as Mother, bless her heart, usually substituted in our defense, *innocence*. You know the old truism, "Ignorance is bliss." If it's so, Len and I may have been the world's biggest blisters, as you are about to see.

"A person who publishes a book appears willfully in public with his pants down."
—Edna St.Vincent Millay

So take cover, hide your eyes, run for the border, or jump right in here with us. We're going to expose our selves.

We hope you'll get accustomed to a heavy use of the plural pronoun "we" in the pages ahead. It isn't literary humility. In most instances, my we's will mean Len—my identical twin brother—and me.

From the first Len was always there. Right up to my honeymoon he was there. Once the honeymoon was over, I said, "Len, now look, don't you th...."

Much more about Len as we go along.

First, one more reminder that when you see and feel our ignorance, our gullibility, naivete or pain, note that we will be laughing. Use any sorrow you feel as your free pass for another good laugh with us.

One time we (there's ole Len again) were working in the fields when Len suddenly threw his hoe down and began running and writhing and grabbing and screaming in obvious pain. Our dad, wise in the ways of the woods and sandy fields, quickly picked Len up and shook and brushed him violently until the little stinging scorpion fell from Len's pants leg. Len, never having seen a scorpion before, stopped crying immediately and calmly said, "It was only a lizard."

Relieved and amazed, Daddy and I asked Len, "Are you all right?"

"Yes," Len said, "It was painful, but it didn't hurt."

That's exactly the way the life I report here was. It was painful, but it didn't hurt.

Some family and friends who read the early drafts of these stories have rushed to me in defense of Len, suggesting that I have been unfair to him, made him the butt of everything. Even my publisher says we should give Len a chance to respond to all the blame and belittling he suffers in these pages.

After a *fair* and *unbiased* review of the material, I failed to note any unfairness. I reject the accusations and have developed a list of seven hundred and eighty-one good, persuasive responses to them. In the interest of space, I have listed below only a few, selected at random.

If after reading these samples, you are not impressed with my fairness to Len and 100 percent on my side in this matter, send a self-addressed,* stamped envelope, and $549.49 for handling to me in care of the publisher

*I will buy a ticket to see an envelope address itself.

and I'll send you the other seven hundred and seventy-seven fool-proof arguments. Or for only $7.74 and all he can eat, I will get a leash and bring Len to your home for a reading.

Here are some examples of my fairness:

(1) I gave Len the leading role in this book, except of course, for my part as "Hero, Governor, Counsellor, Prince of Peace." It's my book, yet Len's name is mentioned many more times than mine is. I'll play his role in his book, should he ever learn to write.

(2) Nitpickers ask, "Were you, as you claim, always the hero, the twin who got everything right, the one who always knew better?" Leaning heavily on my Watergate lessons in the value of a truthful response, my answer is, "Yes, to the best of my recollection I was."

(3) Fairness itself has led me to assign all the credits to me. Let me explain. Stories have abounded in our family since we were infants about how there were several total mix-ups of who was who and which was which. (Our names before baptism were Who and Which or Which and Who.) So just let us imagine that in two or three of the stories that follow we should write Len up as the hero. The odds are good that the Len we let win would, in reality, be the original Ben. So there you would be, heaping still more accolades on my shoulders. Would that be fair?

Or, for all we know, I am ghost writing this book for Len and using Ben as my nom de plume. Or I am Len using the nom de plume of Ben and ghosting it for myself who in this instance is actually Ben.

As any fair reader will conclude, it's better my way. I'll bet even Len will agree to that—but he may be Ben.

(4) Len, nee Which, is happy with this arrangement. After all, he's an identical twin to the star in everyone of these stories. That's not a bad achievement for a guy like Len, if any.

One of the things that distinguishes the human species from among the other animals is our ability to laugh at ourselves—and even at those we hold most dear, *especially* those we hold most dear.

In my life that person has always been ole Len. Or is it Ben?

Finally this note for those among you—and I am told it's a vast majority in the population as a whole—who have fantasized about writing a book: it is as thrilling as you ever thought it would be.

Yet as delightful as this is to me, the book is not for me. It is for you, the individual, one-of-a-kind reader. The only way I can feel fulfilled by the publication of this book is for you to be touched and thrilled and lifted by reading it.

My experience will be bittersweet unless you can find your story among ours and laugh again at yourself, and at Len, and at me—unless we can all recall, laugh, and rejoice together.

So join the celebration. And remember: "It may be painful, but it won't hurt."

Ben Burton
10 Queens Row
Hot Springs, Arkansas 71901
August 14, 1992

FAMILY

Sugarfoot's School of Spit, Polish, and Dance

Sugarfoot (not her real name or foot), my older sister, has never received the fame she's due. She has two reasons to be famous: (1) she may have originated the widely acclaimed Head Start program and (2) invented one of the popular dance steps of the 50s.

Teaching was Sugarfoot's forte. She was born and driven to teach. Even as a youngster, she was forever teaching someone, or something, how to do chores and tricks or how to behave.

She was good at it. Sugarfoot had all the virtues of a good teacher: commitment, patience, firm-but-fair rules. And she didn't eat a lot.

Sugarfoot had taught our pets and farm animals about all they could handle. Did anyone else's cows go outside the stall to "do it," each in its own neat pile? Ours did.

Now Sugarfoot felt ready to teach the basics, including grooming and manners, to a slightly higher form of animal life—her pre-school twin brothers. She was a Mount Everest of pedagogic ambition.

With the permission and backing of our mother, the Sugarfoot School opened. Daily classes were held—where else?—in the "class" room. (Actually it was a seldom-used spare bedroom with little class or room, a place we had always called the junk room.)

School met daily at 5 p.m. after Miss Burton (not her real name either, but she made us call her that during "school") got home from her real school in town. We met daily for one hour, but it was longer than most hours.

Len and I had to dress for class each day and pass Miss Burton's rigid inspection. Grooming received a strong emphasis at old SSSP&D—particularly neat hair. Miss Burton wanted every hair in place. She used a big stiff brush to get our heads slicked down and ready before she would start. This is probably where Head Start got its name.

That brush made a lasting impression on me. Years later, I think I can still feel those stiff bristles gouging into my scalp. Len and I blame that daily brushing for our thinning hair today.

However Sugarfoot's school wasn't just a finishing school. It was also like real school with paper, pencils, assignments, discipline, etc.

Attendance was perfect. We lived in the school house. We would have had to run away from home to miss a day of school. We considered it but could never get organized.

Teacher pupil ratio was excellent—one to two. So we made a lot of progress on a broad front. Naturally I don't remember a lot of specifics of what we learned, but one thing comes to mind—state capitals. This was one of Sugarfoot's long suits and we learned the capitals well. For example, Bismarck is North and Pierre is South. Studies show that more than half the people, even counting those in the Dakotas, don't know that. Thanks, Miss Burton, for making me above average.

Sugarfoot's other claim to fame was the invention of the famous dance, or rag, which bears her name. Like so many historic events, this one took place quite by accident.

My sister, in addition to being a wonderful teacher, was a great candy maker—notably fudge. She made fudge often, but not often enough for Len and me.

We didn't have the language to express it then, but we were addicted to, hooked on, and junkies for fudge—and criminal in our pursuit of it. We would often dive into a pan of fudge before it was even cool and eat far more than our share.

Sugarfoot's kitchen skill and Len's and my greed clashed one day and jarred history into motion. This red letter day, Sugarfoot—nee Miss Burton—was making fudge. Len and I knew it and she knew we knew it and we knew she knew that we knew it. That's the kind of close knit family we were. However she, being older and wiser, had a plan to thwart our mischief.

When the fudge was done and we two young fudge lords were temporarily out of the kitchen, Sugarfoot made her move. She quickly poured the hot brown ooze into two pans and hustled them into the dark pantry and placed them on the floor out of our sight and hers. She could easily guard the one pantry door. She felt triumphant.

Then she heard noises outside. "The pantry window!" Sugarfoot had forgotten the small pantry window and "the little fudge-loving brats were climbing in the window to get their fudge fix!" Sugarfoot dashed into the dark closet to repel the invasion and secure the window. But she forgot the fudge on the floor. She planted first one bare foot and then the other into a pan of blistering hot fudge.

Sugarfoot's wail sent distant neighbors to their storm cellars and dogs scurrying for cover under houses. It stripped every leaf off our mulberry tree just outside. But Sugarfoot's bellow was nothing compared to her dance. With a pan of hot fudge firmly stuck on each foot and a compelling urge to use all her moving parts at once, she then and there earned her nickname and invented the original Sugarfoot rag.

Sugarfoot was not badly injured I'm happy to report. She's still my sister and has lived to laugh with the rest of us over the incident. If she is collecting any royalty from the dance or the tune by the same name or from Head Start, she is concealing the wealth well and maintaining her modest ways.

Sugarfoot never became an actual teacher, but she went on to become one of the world's greatest mothers. By the way, her sons' hair is thinning, much like ours, but they know all the state capitals.

And for you who wondered, yes, of course, we ate the fudge.

All the Comforts
of Nome

Last winter let me down hard. It was one of the mildest ever recorded and I sure was disappointed. I was all primed and hoping for a real winter, the kind we had when I was growing up.

How long has it been since you've had a coating of snow dust down through the shingles at night and your hair stiffened as you slept? How many of you have sung and laughed with your brother or sister through chattering teeth? Len and I chattered a great "Stars and Stripes Forever." Len was better than some on that runaway piccolo part.

Or how long has it been since you've had one of your parents tuck a warm brick under the covers up next to your cold feet. I never felt more loved than then. Parents don't have that opportunity much any more, and it's hard to replace it when it comes to expressing love.

My theory and firm belief is that it's good for us all to be really cold once in a while in our life. Gives us something to lean against and something to look forward to—back on, as well. That old house we lived in when we were growing up provided those advantages. So much cold and so many warm memories.

My wife and I recently built a new home and paid a lot of extra money to have a wood burning fire place put in it. You know that's what people do now days even in the best houses. Why we had a wood burning fireplace in that old house we lived in years ago. We were way ahead of our time. Of course we didn't have central heat to keep the fire place warm. I wasn't warm on both sides at once until I went to college.

That old fireplace of ours must have been a good one. It sure burned a lot of wood. I was twelve years old before I found out my name wasn't "Go get some wood."

Quilts were necessities, not just conversational items. A winter night was measured by the number of quilts it took to survive it. "A four-quilt night back in '98" was a favorite embellishment for one of the great tales my Daddy told. A three-quilter was the worse winter night I remember. That night is memorable, not for the cold, but for the two or three warm brick exchanges that occurred just at the right time.

My wife recently bought a patchwork quilt. It's nice, but it's only decorative. I doubt we will ever have to use it to keep warm. I don't remember that we called our quilts patchwork quilts growing up at Logan's Chapel, but we had patchwork sheets.

The fertilizer we used in the fields came in cloth bags in those days. After they were empty, my mother would wash them, stitch them together, and make sheets out of them. They were nicer than most sheets. We could lie in bed at night and read the sheets: "5-10-5, Nitrate of Soda, Nitrogen." These were among the first words we learned

to read. "Potash," too, but that word never came in handy. I keep looking for a place to use it.

Modesty prevents me from telling you what else Mother made out of those fertilizer sacks. However if they had been selling fertilizer in paper bags in those days, Len and I would have frozen to death in the winter time.

I read a poem not long ago in which the poet said something along the lines of "The rain on the roof at night was like music to my ears." Well when it rained at night in that old house we lived in and after Mother got up and put the pots and pans under all the leaks, it really was like music: "bong, bing, bong, pling." Water dropped like that all over the house. It was kind of musical if your ear wasn't really good. However before I could get Len up to help me keep the pans tuned, the rain usually stopped. Also there was no rhythm to it at all.

There were leaks in the walls and floor as well. One time our city cousin Carroll was visiting us from Pine Bluff. After we had been in bed a while and the talking and giggling had about run down, Len got up and quietly knelt down beside the bed. Then Carroll got up and knelt down on the other side.

"Carroll, what are you doing," I asked.

"The same thing Len is doing," he answered.

"Mother is sure gonna be mad at you, boy. The knot hole is on Len's side."

Admittedly our house was old and run down, but I never had, or heard, a complaint about it. And it was paid for. Or that's what the people who rented it to us claimed.

What we lacked in housing, we made up for in good food and pride. I remember one time Uncle Acey on my

Daddy's side dropped in for supper, unexpected and unannounced as usual. Mother soon retreated to the kitchen and got really busy. She loved to cook but disliked surprises, particularly from my Daddy's side. Supper was called and Mother presented her surprise—a huge bowl of something, all piled up and steaming. It was a one-dish meal.

The ever-eager Uncle Acey asked, "What is that?"

"Rabbit heads and collards," Mother answered. "Here, have some. Just take durn near all of it."

Acey did, but he left earlier than usual. He didn't come back as often either.

"Poor but proud" was coined to describe us. Mother was the source of this sustaining pride. She never despaired out loud and always talked to us as if better was just around the bend. And it always was, and is, even until this day. Mother would not let us feel sorry for ourselves, and she worked regularly on our pride.

I remember when we started to school, a brown paper bag quickly became a status symbol. I hoped someday to carry my lunch to school in a brown paper bag like some of our classmates did. However we didn't have any brown paper bags because we never bought anything in the store. Mother would wrap our lunch up in two pages out of the *Progressive Farmer*, neatly tie it with string, and as she handed it to us, say, "Here, boys. Poor white trash takes it in a bucket." What a booster!

It worked for us. I remember one time Len and I drove a pipe up in our front yard so the neighbors would think we had running water. We just wasted that effort because most of our neighbors didn't know what running water was.

I started this piece out by saying that I regret we didn't have a harder winter. It got me to thinking about that old house we grew up in. If it hadn't finally fallen down, our old house may have, by now, been on the National Register of Historic Places. That old house may have been the place about which someone wrote, "It's not a house that makes a home."

No, a house doesn't make a home, but I know several things that do. One of them is the reason I was yearning for an extra cold winter last year. I was all set for it with our new fireplace, a lot of wood—and a plan.

My plan was to wait until it got really cold one night, new fireplace and all. After everyone turned in, I was going to flip the central heat off and help the house get as cold as our old house used to get. Maybe I would even open a window or two to let some of the winter get inside like it did back then.

I was going to get up in that cold house and warm an old brick I've kept for this purpose. When the brick got just right, I was going to wrap it in a piece of flannel cloth and ease it under the covers and up to my granddaughter's tiny feet.

Even after she has lived as long as I have, she will never feel any more loved than she will at that moment. And that warm memory will bond her forever to me and to our house. That will be good for her—and great for me.

Maybe next year.

All Around the Radio with the Great Americans

"There are more bores around now than when I was a boy."

Fred Allen spoke that jewel on the radio. Today he might say it about radio. If he doesn't, I will.

If I have to quote Fred Allen, I'll have to break a promise I made to myself fifty some-odd years ago. I decided then that I was going to avoid ever saying anything superlative about "the good ol' days," like "this and that being much better back when I was growing up."

For one thing Mother and Daddy, as good as they were, wore those viewpoints out grinding them into us when we were growing up—our grandparents, too. For another, I just never have believed that things were ever better than right now. Mostly I still don't.

However one thing was a whole lot better when we were growing up than it is now—radio. When I say radio was better back then, I don't mean the radio itself was better. It definitely was not better—relatively more expensive, but not better. It was hard to hear an old radio. When you can't hear a radio, it doesn't have much left to hold your interest. It's about like listening to a big cigar box. Len can tell you how dull that gets after an hour or two.

What do I mean when I say radio was better when we were growing up? I mean radio as a respected institution, as a central force in life. It was much better, much stronger than today. The personalities on the radio were more talented. Those good enough to be on the radio were really good, celebrities. There were not nearly as many stations as today to thin out the talent, not within your hearing range anyway. One was lucky to get even one station clearly, not counting Del Rio, Texas, blasting in most of the time, coming through faintly even on an otherwise dead battery.

Len said he could hear Del Rio without a radio by cupping his ears and facing the southwest. However he hardly ever did it, said what he heard wasn't worth the trouble. The only time the family ever listened to Del Rio on purpose was when we had a failing battery, which was often, or when we needed to brush up on our Spanish, which was rarely.

I think this lack of choice made it easier for the programs we could get to be good. Much of the programming was network programming, not local. The programs were staffed by memorable people. There was no pimply-faced, adenoidal school boy who "boys" the microphone, says "git," "crish-chul," and "Westconsin."

Fred Allen had this figured way back.

The voices we heard on the radio belonged to real *face-cards*—giants. They were people whose names we knew, whose voices we recognized, and whose word we took—

people like Harry VonZell, H. V. Kaltenborn, Don Wilson, Ben Grauer, Gabriel Heatter, Walter Winchell, and "all the ships at sea."

Surely you understand that I am talking about *country* radio. Oh, probably some of you don't. Think you do, but you don't. When I say country radio, I'm not talking about all those country stations from one end of the dial to the other. It seems that half or more of the many stations I can hear today are country stations or say they are, even some up North. Well I'm not talking about country stations like those. What I mean is a radio *in* the country.

It may be difficult for some to imagine what a dominant influence a tiny, battery powered radio was to the rural family in the thirties. Radio *united* families then like television *unties* them today. For one thing, a family was forced to sit really close to the radio and therefore to each other in order to hear it. This was particularly true when the battery began to fade, which was usually right after we had it charged.

Radio was better than television in other ways also. You had to get involved in radio because each listener had to be providing his own pictures all the time. "Be quiet, Len. Don't you see Cedric coming up on the porch with his lantern?"

Another thing helped radio. We weren't always losing or fighting over the remote control. There was no remote, and few controls. All listeners were within easy reach of each other and the controls—two small knobs on our set.

Women and children were not allowed to operate the controls in our house. It took a "technician" like Dad to manage a radio through an evening of listening. Not everybody could keep the tuner straddle of the distant station when Del Rio was trying to butt in. This was usually worse just before one of Joe Louis' knockdowns.

"Who was it? Which one? Who got knocked down?"

I don't know why we asked. In Louis' fights, it was always the other guy.

When we would begin losing our signal or getting more Del Rio than we could stand, Dad would have to take matters into his own hands—literally. Accustomed to working with mules, Dad would pound his fist on just the right place with just the right force at just the right time to clear things up temporarily—always temporarily.

Dad's fine tuning technique was largely lost when electricity came in. I'm going to try his method on my big flashlight the next time I go frog gigging.

Radio bonded us not just physically but in common celebrations, causes, and contests. Programs like "Your Hit Parade," "Dr. I.Q.," and the second Max Schmeling fight nourished our family esprit de corps better even than grits. Talk about family togetherness, the world needs to re-invent radio.

Our family loved radio. But that feeling wasn't unanimous in the neighborhood. Our Uncle Jim Gunter never believed in radio.

"Do you mean to tell me, boys, that from a box with wires on it and me a-sittin' in your livin' room, I can hear people a-talkin' in New York City? And a-singin' and a-fightin' and all that? I'll never believe it.

"Yore Daddy's been out in the heat too much lately if he's a-tellin' you them kinda things. There ain't no way that could work, boys. It'd be entirely unnatural."

Even after we talked Uncle Jim into coming over and listening to part of one of Joe Louis' fights, he didn't believe it. After cupping his hand around his ear through three rounds and letting out one big "soooooie, pig!" when Joe knocked Primo Carnera down, Uncle Jim got up, put his hat on, and left proclaiming, "Naw, I still don't believe it. Work of the devil is what it is."

It's hard to counter that kind of reasoning. We didn't try. We knew what worked for us.

Mr. President

President Franklin Delano Roosevelt was a member of our family, or that's the way it felt. Radio was the reason for that feeling.

President Roosevelt had a masterful radio voice, and he visited with us often. He would call us all together in what he called a fireside chat. I wondered about his need for a fire during some of those. Who knows what goes on up North?

It's difficult for my children, and a world of others born after the great depression, to understand the reverence with which most households held President Franklin Delano Roosevelt. To this day, Presidents fall into two groups for many of us of that era. President Roosevelt is in one group, and all the others are not.

We may have let our loyalty to President Roosevelt go too far. Len and I felt responsible for the terrible thing that happened to Governor Alf Landon in the election of 1936. We didn't stuff any ballot boxes or bribe any judges or anything like that, but we did pull hard against Governor Landon. We hoped and prayed some as well. We just couldn't understand why anyone in America would try to take President Roosevelt's job away from him. We held that against Governor Landon and fervently wanted President Roosevelt to win and win big. We weren't prepared for the success we had.

I remember our grieving together about how sad Governor Alf Landon must be after the terrible beating he took in the election. Oh, we never were for Governor Landon. We just felt bad that he got beat so bad and that maybe our being so strong for President Roosevelt had something to do with it. Mr. Kaltenborn said Governor Landon got only six votes. Six votes! Good gracious, all of his own family must not have voted for him. How humiliating that must have been for him.

Of course people invariably say, "Oh, well. Those were electoral votes."

Even so, six is six. We didn't understand the electoral college then and a few people still don't understand it. I don't have room or time here to explain it.

For a long time Len and I felt bad about what we did to Governor Landon. Mother said Governor Landon was probably a fine man, a fellow farmer. And just six votes! Len and I wondered if he went out to his barn up there in Kansas and cried. We cried a little, not that we wanted him to win. But just six votes!

We sure never wanted President Roosevelt to know that we made it up to the Republicans during their convention four years later. Len and I sat around the radio and joined in on the "We Want Wilkie" chant night after night until he got the nomination. We celebrated just like we were Republicans, but we kept it to ourselves.

We didn't want Wilkie to win either. However we sure didn't want another Landon on our conscience. As you know, Wilkie lost, but I believe he got more than six votes.

Last fall I was delighted and thrilled to meet United States Senator Nancy Landon Kassebaum, the late Governor's daughter. She was nice to me, but somehow I felt like she knew. I tried to talk mostly about wheat. I sure didn't want to slip up and ask her if she was one of the six.

The Early Invasion of Columbia County

Recent wars have been, as the saying goes, "brought into our living rooms" by television. I've heard it claimed that this made war even worse. I know the person who said they had never seen a war on radio. A war can be a lot worse when you have to make up your own pictures.

As a child, I overheard on my aunt's radio that Nazi Germany was marching into Poland. I had no idea where Poland was. The man on the radio sounded excited and Poland looked close in my pictures. I went running home to Mother wondering every step if I could get there before Hitler and his tanks came clanking and grinding over the horizon. Len fell down laughing at me. He said Poland was clear on the other side of Haynesville in North Louisiana and Hitler couldn't get here for at least a week. Len lucked out again.

The scene is also clear in my memory and feelings when President Roosevelt called us all together and told us about Pearl Harbor. We knew he would tell us what to do—and he did. And we did what he said gladly. We accepted it—rationing, the draft, paper drives, all that—

without any question, including black-outs. With our two coal oil lamps, the black-outs weren't much of a sacrifice.

"Glad to, Mr. President," we all said in unison. I liked feeling that way about the President.

One of the worst wars during this period hasn't happened yet. We heard our folks whispering about hearing Orson Wells on the radio describing the coming "War of the Worlds." They sounded scared. It was enough to give us nightmares. I never got the details or the due date straight, but it won't hurt to keep your shades drawn at night and a pitch fork handy. I do.

Even some of the entertainment shows were emotional for us because we would get so involved. For example, Len and I would sometimes cry with the poor soul who got the gong on Major Bowes' "Original Amateur Hour." We pictured his family huddled around a radio out there somewhere, upset and carrying on because Bubba Ray got the gong in the first twenty seconds of his act. We decided kind and gentle ole Major Bowes just didn't like Bubba Ray or the way he played the spoons and the hand saw at the same time, Bubba Ray being one-armed and all.

Len and I dreamed a lot about being on the Major Bowes' show. The dream kept us working on our duet of "I'm An Ol' Cowhand From the Rio Grande." Only the fear of getting the gong in under twenty seconds kept us off. Maybe someday we'll risk it. We are still in rehearsal, and Len is getting more bow legged all the time.

Our older brother Don was musical, so he loved Kate Smith, a great singer of that era. She sang "God Bless America" so well that she ruined it for every other singer for all time. My brother used to say that when he finished high school, he was going to go to New York City and marry Kate Smith. He did, in fact, go to New York City, but he didn't marry Kate Smith. When he saw Kate Smith, he found out that radio is even blinder than love.

We had a lot of electronic evangelists even back then. Their pitch was about like now except that in exchange for your donation they would actually send you something, a special "Cosmic Connector" pad you could kneel on while touching your radio and thereby "close the connection" with the evangelist's microphone. (Len used to constantly embarrass me by pronouncing this word "microphoney." He may have been on to something.)

I see the lottery results from time to time on television. We didn't have lotteries on radio, but we had something far better and more dependable: the coupon saving contests. We saved a few of each of the coupons available but never got enough to cash in on one of the prizes.

I have let Len manage our collection since we left home. He's been trading our coupons the way some trade baseball cards. If Len has managed it right and the big *Ovaltine* offer ever comes back, we're gonna be sitting pretty for a bus trip to the New York World's Fair. We've been waiting to go to the World's Fair for years. We saw it on our radio in 1936. I bet you haven't seen or heard of anything like the *Ovaltine* offer or the New York World's Fair on your radio lately.

Fred Allen saw this coming a long time ago.

Doctor Cries Fowl!

Both of my parents were award winning doctors.

Mother and Dad—we didn't call them Doctor at home—had a thriving practice. With six children, the usual farm animal menagerie, and several sickly neighbors, they had all the business they could handle—along with running the farm. Their medical practice was a necessary sideline and the awards they won were intangible.

If one has to be technical, I must admit that Mother and Dad weren't *actual* doctors. However they were the only doctors available to us, and they were healers. To us, that made them doctors.

My parents were conscientious doctors. They even made house calls. In fact all their work was house calls. Well some calls were barn calls, but that's a house call from one point of view. And some were hospital calls. A hospital is what our house became the year we all had whooping cough, chicken pox, and ring worms right in a row.

My parents were *specialists*—specialists in everything. (This made them oxymorons also long before that word reached our area. They would have been so proud.)

Mother and Dad handled all the specialties. And you couldn't tell they were doing it. They flowed so smoothly one to another: Internal, Psychiatry, Veterinary, Rehabilitation, Psychology, Pharmacy, Dermatology, Podiatry, Dentistry, Ophthalmology... with also, a blend of Hypnosis and Anesthesiology called "Think About Something Else," which to this day works amazingly well in many medical situations.

And surgery. Yes, surgery. Bloodless surgery at that. Many times I heard the Doctors say, "If this boy's boil is not better by tomorrow, we will have to lance it!" However they never had to. Magically, the boil would erupt or retreat overnight. I never knew if they had a lance. They never needed one.

Examples and actual cases from the endless list of Doctors Burtons' wonder drugs, potions, practices, and reasonable facsimiles:

Coal Oil, the Cure-All

Coal oil was a double misnomer. "Coal oil," our lamp fuel, was actually kerosene, a petroleum derivative, and "Coal oil," our lamp fuel, was actually our world's first wonder drug. It may still be. Nobody much uses it anymore—penicillin is such a catchy name.

Among the many things our "doctors" applied coal oil to were scrapes, acne, tedder, bruises, punctures, sprains, strains, hurt feelings, scratches, insect bites (prevention and treatment), poison oak, poison ivy, stone bruises (a deep, major league heel bruise known only to bare footed boys and impossible to describe to others), leg ache, foot ache, heart ache, saddle sores, home sickness, and sore throat (just a drop with sugar).

Side Effects:

Slightly unpleasant odor could last up to a week or until your next bath, whichever came first.

Advantages:

Always immediately available.

Inexpensive: most effective when mixed with prayer and applied by or to believers.

Palm Oil and Hair for Splinters and Briars

Recently a man told me he went to the hospital to have a splinter removed from his finger. While there for the surgery, he had a heart attack. What a waste and a shame that he didn't know about Dad's course of treatment.

Dad would gently ease a splinter or briar out with tweezers or the blade of his pocket knife, place the briar or splinter in your hand, and tell you with a convincing faith to "rub it in your hair and it won't even get sore." It never did. Try this on your next briar or splinter. When it works, give a loving smile and a non-judgmental greenback to the next street person you see. This is the same kind of healing. It works alike for healee and healer.

Side Effects:

Removal may be slightly painful; not watching the operation plus laughing uproariously during process helps; following blackberry picking could lead to a brief siege of painful, black dandruff.

Advantages:

May prevent heart attacks; inexpensive.

Special Tip:

Works best when combined with well known coal oil treatment.

Soot and/or Spider Webs for Clotting

Not for the squeamish, this proven method of controlling free bleeding would be better known if used more often. One or both elements will work but best if used in combination. Our uncle, when just a boy, could have bled to death after having been kicked in the lip by a horse. Quick action and an extremely sooty lamp globe probably saved his life. While it's true that he went through life with a big black exclamation point on his lip, he lived a long, successful life and never bled again, at least not from the lip.

Side Effects:

Some local discoloring and an aversion to lamp light may occur.

Advantages:

Vastly better than the alternative; may produce men of distinction.

Special Tip:

Works best when followed with the increasingly famous coal oil treatment.

Special Tobacco Preparation for Wasp and Bee Stings:

Wasps and bees were common. So were stings. And they were painful. But if one could get to Dad quickly, before the swelling began, relief and ultimate cure were at hand. Dad carried this medicine with him, in a can in his pocket, to combat wasps—and his own demon. It was the tobacco from which Dad "rolled his own" and worked his magic.

Faced with a wasp or bee sting, his action was swift and

fluid, so to speak. He would pop open the red can (many have identified the brand by now), grab a big pinch of *Prince Albert*, pop it into his mouth, and start the miraculous mastication which changed a curse into a cure. Moments later he would expel the ugly, brown juicy mass into his fingers and gently paste and pat it onto the sting area, accompanied by his low mantra of high expectations. This stopped the sobs of the most tender little child or grandchild within minutes.

Side Effects:

Could lead to Christian Science; never use this medicine around an open flame or put it in your pipe and smoke it.

Advantages:

Only known beneficial use of this product.

Special Tip:

Sting victims with non-smoking doctors should try the world famous coal oil treatment.

Fresh Breast of Chicken for Snake Bite:

Poisonous snake bite was always one of the worst dreads in a rural setting. Thankfully it didn't happen often. Once in a lifetime was about average. Therefore prevention was emphasized heavily. Fear of snakes was implanted early and supplanted often with wild, improbable legends about snakes. However bites did happen occasionally and a treatment was needed.

The old haywire tourniquet method had been discredited as worse than the venom. It sometime worked but at major sacrifice by the victim. Also it was totally ineffective from the neck up.

Ultimately the chicken breast method emerged, the theory being that a fresh chicken breast when held over the bite would draw the venom out. (The drawing power of breasts was recognized even back then.)

We almost had the chance to try the breast method first hand when Dad was bitten by a copperhead while working in the garden. He came in quietly, lay down on the bed, and calmly began to direct his own treatment. Or as my friend Charlie Allbright would say, "He began to put himself into a dying condition."

Dad asked Mother to find his other underwear and to locate and mark with crayon the tiny puncture marks on his lower leg. Len was dispatched to the chicken yard to get a chicken breast. Dad asked me to get pencil and paper and begin writing his will.

In snakebite cases, time is everything. Where was that chicken breast? Len finally returned, empty handed, to report that we didn't have any chickens with breasts. "The chickens out there are all singletons, all males, I guess. Not any breasts in that lot."

Dad swelled a lot and was very sick but survived, chicken breast or not. This was probably because Mother, when she found and marked the punctures, gently dabbed on a thimble full of coal oil.

Side Effects:

Leads to preference for dark meat; hard on the chickens.

Advantages:

Forces one to update the will and to change underwear.

Special Tip:

There is no recorded death from snakebite where enough coal oil was applied soon enough.

Use any of these tested cures you like. No one will call on you at home, and you won't be billed. Some cures are not available in Nebraska or where prevented by law or ignorance.

Although I don't keep a can of *PA* or a sooty lamp or lance ready, we always remember the essence of what the good doctors practiced. When our own children hurt—and now our grandchildren—we react swiftly and positively with the best available care. We lay it on gently with love and assurance. And we believe like everything that it will work.

I know that's what you do as well.

'Scuse me. It's time to go dig some sassafras for my Spring purgative. And I think I'll take along some coal oil in case the chiggers and ticks are out. Can't hurt.

Mother Had a Word for It

Mother died at age ninety never suspecting that she had been afflicted all her life with logophilia and had passed it along to her children. She would have been so proud to have me say that—if I pronounced logophilia right. I'll bet she is laughing about all this right now along with the rest of us.

If by now you have gotten back from where you keep your dictionary, you'll know that logophilia is the "worship of or devotion to words." As incongruous as it seems, our dear, semi-educated, stay-at-home, *Progressive Farmer*-type Mother loved words and our language. She used words colorfully, forcefully, and properly, most of the time, and was attentive to keeping current and improving. Also Mother was not averse to coining a good word when the need arose. Another thing, Mother imprinted her children with her impelling interest in words and language.

Mother was a snob of sorts. She was a kind and tolerant person, if there ever was one, in most areas, but snobbish about a few things: cleanliness, table manners, and above all else speaking correctly, cleanly, and well.

Mother had little formal education. Nevertheless good

and proper speech was supremely important to her. I never had my "mouth washed out with soap and water," but I grew up with a vision of what it might be like and a determination to avoid earning the honor.

Poor grammar was equally offensive to Mother. Often in the wake of it she would assume one of her mocking alteregos and mimic disdainfully one who had abused the language. Hers was not a misplaced pride albeit an unusual one in a setting where there was so little else in which to take pride. It was one of the few rations of culture we could afford, I suppose.

Some of Mother's Most Colorful and Powerful Words and Phrases and How to Properly Use Them

Hard-Down: An emphatic adverb, as in "You boys are just hard-down filthy."

Beads: A strange necklace-like formation of hard-down filth that forms every few minutes around the necks of little boys.

Toe Jam: Hard-down filth that has oozed as far as it can ooze and has distilled into an odorous gum between the toes. Remove only in open air. Never place residue in a small fruit jar.

Gingerbread: You know what this is, as in, "Len, you have gingerbread in your pants again." Never, ever shape into small men or take to your grandmother's house.

Set Your Cap: Set lofty goals and make up your mind to achieve them.

Too Big for Your Britches: Cocky. As in "You may be

getting too big for your britches, young man." Rarely used without "young man." Could also cause gingerbread.

Scarce as Hen's Teeth: Rare or non-existent.

Green as a Gourd: No refinement. Bad grammar.

Lick and a Promise: Poor performance or uncompleted task.

Mother often used the following two expletives which follow. Use your own judgement around children.

I'llbejohnnybrown: As in, "Well, I'll be Johnny Brown. You through already? You sure you didn't just give those beads a lick and a promise?"

Yessireebobtail: As in "Yes siree, bobtail, you are going to take another bath. You are hard-down filthy."

The body of language existing then couldn't always accommodate Mother's exuberance, color, and need for oxprossion. That didn't stop her. She added richly to the language.

I didn't take down or try to remember all of Mother's original words and phrases. By the time I realized that she was creating a new vocabulary, many of the words were gone.

Below are a few of Mother's words that you won't find in the dictionary, but you may find useful sometime. I sure do.

Joopus or Joobus: Suspicious of or afraid of.

Querled: Reference to a snake ready to strike. Accompanied by the serpentine movement of arms and the rapid flicking of the tongue. Perhaps hybridized from "coiled" and "curled." Has caused gingerbread in some cases.

Quarn Crow: As "Those socks smell like pure dee quarn crow." Perhaps mongrelized from carrion crow.

Scrooch Up: A winter word meaning curl up, cuddle up, get closer to stay warm.

A Top Water: A shallow or phoney character.

And these originals from Mother's kitchen:

Flop: A recipe or dish that didn't turn out as planned.

Flash: A bad flop Mox: An extra bad flop.

Mox: An extra bad flop.

Maxi Mox: A mox when company was coming.

Even a mox was always delicious to Len and me.

Mother wanted to speak well, worked at it, and was correct most of the time. However she was uneasy with some words, particularly around certain people, like my Uncle Anson (if any) who, when he listened—which was rarely—listened aggressively. He would examine and probe what you were saying, as you said it, and even correct your pronunciation, as you pronounced it. Mother was uneasy and unsure around him and would always plan and rehearse the things she might get to say or might have to say around Uncle Anson.

While in college, I had an emergency appendectomy. Mother visited me in the hospital. On her return trip home, it was convenient for her to route back by way of Uncle Anson's. She knew he would ask about the surgery, so she began intensive preparation. She rehearsed and rehearsed *"a-pend-dec´-to-my, a-pend-dec´-to-my, a-pend-dec´-to-my,"* in order to be ready for the inquisition. The question came early, as Mother knew it would. She was nervous but practiced and ready for a fast answer.

"Well, Evalee, what kind of surgery did you say Ben had?"

"A *hysterectomy*," my over-anxious Mother fired back. Uncle Anson was not amused. Mother let it go as a joke anyway and proudly told us later that at least she pronounced hysterectomy correctly—"before a tough audience too!"

Logophilia afflicts across a broad spectrum—all word forms. Mother was interested in names—people names and places names—and playful with them, as well, for which I am particularly grateful. She had a collection of supposedly authentic names she would recite to us for amusement purposes.

Mother often told us the name of the man who lived and farmed on their place when she was growing up: Tommafa, Ditifa, Christopher, Holmes, Peterfer, Wallopher, Henry Jones. Fortunately, he chose to be called Henry Jones, or simply T.D.C.H.P.W.H. Jones.

Mother usually coupled this story with one told by her Mother. Mamma Smith said that when she started to school in the 1860s, there was a bashful boy in her class who rarely said anything. Day after day when the teacher asked for his name, the timid lad answered simply, "Thomas." After several days, the teacher insisted, "Thomas, don't you have another name?"

Thomas girded up his courage and said, "My name is

Thomas, Dittimus, Catimus, Button-Ping Billington."

After restoring order, the teacher responded, "Isn't that an unusual name, Thomas?"

She wasn't ready for his answer. "No, Ma'am. My brothers are named Memphis, Camden, and Railroad."

One of Mother's most powerful words wasn't a word at all but a melody, a one-note tune that would strike like lightening in Len's and my ears when we had over-stayed our agreed-upon time to be home. The arresting sound was Mother's extremely shrill whistle done fortissimo with no fingers.

Mother's single loud blast meant, "I mean right now, boys." We had been warned to "never make me whistle twice." We never tested that warning.

Mother probably never ran across the word logophilia, but she was a confirmed devotee. I'm thankful she willed that interest to us. However it's more than words that communicate. The music also makes a difference, and the instrument that plays it. Words count, yes, but the life and feelings behind them impact at least as much. Most of us use the word love. Love was Mother's favorite word, and she used it often. In addition, she lived the word.

"Recite with me now, boys, *'Though I speak with the tongues of men and of angels and have not Love, I am become as sounding brass or a tinkling cymbal; And though I have the gift of prophecy and....'*"

Mother has been gone for twelve years. I lived away from home for decades before that, yet she still inspires, teaches, and leads me every day. Is that a strong communicator, or what?

Mother had a word for it.

Was Ab Normal?

My late Daddy is indescribable. I spend a lot of time trying to describe him, like now. Yet he is indescribable. However I won't settle for that. And I hope you won't either.

Daddy wasn't dumb, just different. Daddy wasn't marching to a different drummer. I think Daddy was marching to the fife, or maybe the flag. I know he was hearing a different beat from the rest of us, or flutist.

We laughed a lot in our family. Daddy would laugh too, if we told him it was a joke. Otherwise he put a serious value and face on everything.

Abner Doubleday Burton. That was Daddy's full name. Everyone called him Ab. I asked Daddy many times— until he just wore me down evading it—if he was kin to the inventor of baseball.

"Never knew much about baseball, son," he always answered. "We played Town Ball when I was growing up." I never learned anything about Town Ball either because Daddy always followed that answer with his invention stories.

"Naw, son, all I ever invented was the helicopter."

"Oh?" I would challenge as I got older. "I thought a guy named Sikorsky or Seversky invented the helicopter."

"Well, yeah, maybe later," Daddy would say earnestly.

Len and I would poke each other and whisper, "Is Ab normal?" Daddy didn't hear us because he would be continuing on to tell again about his life long interest in and work on *perpetual motion*—interest in and thought, mostly. It was hard for a two-mule Arkansas cotton farmer to do a lot of actual work on perpetual motion—or helicopters.

Our farm was near a tiny little community named Logan's Chapel in southwest Arkansas—now gone completely back to nature. I asked Daddy one time how he managed to settle at Logan's Chapel. "Oh, well," he said, "Logan's Chapel is a fine little community, a wonderful place to live and farm." I assured him I knew that but persisted in my question of how he chose it.

"Why, it's right here in the middle of the surrounding territory," was his unimpeachable, closing answer. Len and I giggled and asked each other, "Is Ab normal?"

In conversation Daddy had a habit I called *branching*. It got worse, or better (?), as he grew older. He would start out on one subject and quickly branch to another, then another, and another without reaching the end of any story.

I remember one time I was home after I was grown. Daddy greeted me with excitement and said, "Son, I'm sure glad you're here. Did you hear about the terrible thing that happened to the middle Burdine boy?" My quizzical look told him that I had not heard.

Daddy said, "You remember the Burdines, don't you? They used to make our syrup. They are not making syrup anymore. They are making something though. Using a

bunch of jars and sugar. They had better watch out. They'll end up in the pen like the Paschals. You remember the Paschals, don't you?"

I want to remember the Paschals in the worse way so we can get back to the terrible thing that happened to the Burdine boy.

"Was Mr. Paschal a tall, thin man with a moustache?" I asked.

Daddy puzzled briefly and answered in deadpan, "Son, if Paschal wore a moustache, he kept it shaved off."

While I tried untangling that one, he branched ahead.

"I think you are thinking of the Talleys. You surely remember the Talleys."

"Big family over west of us that had all the odd children?" I asked, trying to fight off my impatience.

"Naw, son," Daddy responded. "You're thinking of the Walthalls. The Talleys didn't have any children to speak of. They had all those fine coon dogs. Still do. I heard that one of those dogs struck a trail at Nation's Creek last Wednesday and treed on Friday up close to Mena."

By now we are four families and five counties away from where we started. I'm itching to get back to the original story, so I ask, "Yes, Daddy, what about the middle Burdine boy?"

With wide innocent eyes Daddy said, "Oh, did you know him?" Was Ab normal? Stay tuned.

When I coached football in Texas, I worked with a coach who had a very colorful expression I had never heard anyone else use. He often said, particularly when he was exasperated with a player, "Well I'll be a suck egg mule." I had shared that story many times, usually to mild amusement at least.

Once Daddy was visiting me, and we had about run out of things to talk about: inventions, moustaches, coon dogs, etc. I remembered my suck egg mule story and thought it would be a natural for Daddy, he being an old mule man himself. Daddy got attentive when I told him that I was working with a coach who had an unusually colorful expression I had never heard before. "Yeah," he said, "What's that?"

When I told him Coach Underwood was always saying, "Well I'll be a suck egg mule!" Daddy didn't crack a smile. He appeared thoughtful and I worried, "Uh oh, here comes perpetual motion again."

Then Daddy spoke, continuing with my general education and yours, "Well, son, I don't believe I ever heard of a suck egg mule, but we once had a horse that ate little chickens."

At least he didn't say as he once did to Len in a conversation like this, "And who did you say you are, sir?"

Was Ab normal? Probably not.

Is dropping everything at any time and patiently giving quality time to his children and grandchildren normal? Is getting on one's knees at bedtime every night of your life to say thanks when there was so little visible to say thanks for normal?

Was Ab normal? Probably not.

Is loving everybody in the whole world and refusing to carry grudges normal?

Daddy often said and always practiced these words, "Son, hate is a burden a strong man can't bear."

My Daddy, a strong **Ab**normal man!

He Was the Kind of Grandad That I Want to Be

For Ab and Daddy B

He was a pal, both funny and sage;
A teacher and a play mate, forever my age.
He showed me my best side and how great life can be;
And that's the kind of Grandad I wanna be.

He taught me to whittle, to fish and to spit;
And that I'd never lose, if I didn't quit;
How to spin tops and to set a good snare;
And that "hate is a burden a strong man can't bear."
To believe in myself, as he did in me,
And that's the kind of Grandad I wanna be.

He showed me a real man's both tender and tough;
And to hear my inner voice, for all the "right stuff";
He truly believed there's a miracle in me,
And that's the kind of Grandad that I wanna be.

He was big and brave but could think like a child;
He showed me the magic in a leaf and a smile;
He was ready to join in my laugh or my cry;
He modeled how to live—and then, how to die.
So come, my beloveds, and sit on my knee;
'Cause that's the kind of Grandad that I wanna be;

'Cause that's the kind of Grandad, I'm gonna be!

Mother's Tabernacle Choir

The Mormon Tabernacle Choir is a great one. However every time I hear The Mormon Tabernacle Choir do one of those stirring numbers for which they are famous, I always think, "Fine, but I'll bet you are not singing that number in the key of C."

They couldn't have made it in Mother's Choir. In Mother's family choir, we did everything in the key of C. That was the only key Mother could chord the piano in. This produced a mixed blessing. It narrowed our repertoire severely, but on those occasions when we shoehorned a song into C anyway, it provided a good alibi for some horrible bellowing and screeching on the highs and lows.

We sang some "must" songs, like the "Star Spangled Banner," right key or not. We interspersed moments of silence on the notes we couldn't reach. But we were patriotic enough to mouth the words in those places. I see a lot of people doing that at football games. Mute patriots.

You don't hear a lot of moments of silence from the Mormons. They always manage to be in a good key.

Many things bind families together: work, play, meals,

laughter, grief, remembering, listening, talking, and cele-
brating. One other thing stands out on my list—singing.

Mother must have listed singing, too. It sure worked for
our family. She about insisted that at least once a week—
almost every Sunday night—we all get together around
the piano and sing.

Everybody joined in and got to know the songs and each
other better and better. When you are trying to harmonize
in a small group, you get to know each other especially
well. They need you and you need them. Otherwise you're
just left hanging out there on a long note with no one to
cover your flaws. Families don't let that happen to each
other.

Mother's choir became pretty good on a limited program. We did the same songs over and over again each
session, limited to the number of songs we could do in C.
We knew many other songs we could sing in other keys,
but without accompaniment our musical warts showed
bad.

Len and I could play our guitars in other keys, A and G,
which could have provided the group with more song
choices. The trouble was that we only played *twin-method
guitar*. That means while one twin was playing a chord,
the other twin was getting the next chord ready. If he got
it ready in time, he would jump right in on the beat. The
method worked fairly well on slow numbers like "Swing
Low, Sweet Chariot," but on anything faster it produced
fits and starts in the rhythm. The rest of the choir took an
un-Mormon-like attitude about this and voted to dismiss
us from the choir if we played our guitars.

Not only that, it finally sank in on us that it was not a

big compliment when after we played "Fascinating Rhythm" for Aunt Era, she told us "nice young men can play the guitar, but don't."

So it was back to Mother's choir, the piano, the key of C, and our standard fare:

"When the Saints Go Marching In"

"Blessed Assurance"

"The Star Spangled Banner," with gaps

All the songs of Stephen Foster (Occasionally, for variety, we would do non-C songs to the tune of Foster's "Suwannee River." Most numbers didn't sound as good as you might think.)

"Amazing Grace"

"When It's Lamp Lighting Time in the Valley"

"Just a Song at Twilight"

"Blue Heaven"

"Red Wing" (I always hated to see this one coming)

> There once was an Indian maid;
> * * *
> * * *
> Now the moon shines tonight on Pretty Red Wing;
> * * *
> When all the braves returned,
> The heart of Red Wing yearned;
> For far, far away, her warrior gay,
> Fell bravely in the fray.
> Now the moon shines tonight on pretty Red Wing;
> * * *

For reasons better left for psychoanalysis, I associated the brave warrior sadly with our oldest brother Paul in far off New York City. When I sensed that "Red Wing" was coming up on our program, I would find a reason to leave the room, go to the back steps, think of Paul, tear-up and pray a little until "Red Wing" was over. (Len, too.)

These sessions were an intimate ritual, mainly for immediate family. Nevertheless we couldn't be rude to near-flesh and blood. Burmadean Crump, our second or third cousin (anyone counting?) who lived over on the old Talley place about two miles away if you took the trail, crashed the group often.

And could she sing? In a word, "occasionally." Burmadean either choked up around us or just couldn't manage the key of C. Whatever the reason—even allowing for family bias—Burmadean was awful. It was so embarrassing when our dogs under the house started howling the moment Burmadean joined in. We would have to make up a quick coon story to help her save face.

But Burmadean could sing one song well and was famous for it. I mean good enough to sing it out in public—the lovely "Embraceable You." She sang it all over the county. Once Burmadean even did "Embraceable You" for a funeral. "Altered a few of the words," she said.

The best music we ever had was when our older sister Mary Sue came home to visit. She has a trained voice and can sure enough sing. She didn't seem to add much to the choir's "Stouthearted Men," done to the tune of "Suwannee River." However she didn't hurt it either.

About then Mother, who didn't care for our "Stouthearted Men," would give Mary Sue a knowing look and say, "Solo, multi-mosso."

Mary Sue would give Mother a knowing look and say, "Acappella."

I thought it was classy the way they talked Latin to each other that way. Then Mary Sue would goose bump us all by singing "Ave Maria" by herself. I never heard a single familiar word in that song, but the tune sure was pretty. The choir never could learn "Ave Maria." Mary Sue wasn't really disappointed. I don't believe it's in the key of C anyway.

I've deliberately left our biggest and best song until the last, which was something Daddy was rarely able to do. Every time the choir assembled, Daddy would lobby Mother early and long, "Let's do my favorite song, 'When...' "

"Well, wait, Ab. You know we're going to get to it," Mother would appeal.

Daddy would eventually prevail, and we would all join him in his favorite—and our best: "When the Roll Is Called Up Yonder."

Daddy couldn't keep from exuberantly waving his arms and leading us in this one. He would always say as we finished, "I want that one done at my funeral." He said it so unvaryingly that we could lip-sync with him. And it was sung at his funeral.

Mother's Tabernacle Choir still assembles from time to time, without the original leaders, but with some promising apprentices. We still sing the oldies, mostly in the key of C. And we always do "When the Roll Is Called Up Yonder."

There is a strong hint of immortality present.

FUN

The Extraordinary Logan's Chapel Church Zoo

I'm probably not the first person who when confronted face to face with a dirty black 1989 Ford Taurus realized how much it looks like a great big flathead catfish. How many though will also realize, head-on that way, that the Ford Taurus is the spitting image of Mr. Roy Simpkins. I know Len will. Len was the first to recognize it.

But wait, I'm getting things all out of order. Mr. Simpkins had his look first—or second, actually. He preceded the Ford Taurus by fifty years but succeeded the flathead cat by Lord knows how long. But to us he always did look exactly like a big catfish sitting up there in the bass section of the Logan's Chapel Church Choir. Mr. Simpkins had a lot of interesting company in that choir, too.

That Logan's Chapel Church Choir is where Len and I started noticing and cataloging how the individual choir members looked like various animals. Don't tell me you've never noticed it—with your choir I mean. Everybody has done it. Come on now, denial is not good for your mental health.

My sister used to say our doing this was "just awful." I hope not. Len and I didn't do it in a ridiculing way. With us it was an irresistible, natural way of observing and remembering individuals. It was kind of like this: "Animal is in the eye of the beholder." We didn't intend to harm anyone. I contend it's better than not remembering people at all. Do you think I will ever forget Mr. Roy Simpkins? I think of him every time I see a catfish or a Ford Taurus. There's a lot of both out there but only one Roy Simpkins.

This wasn't just some childish game we invented, played a while and forgot. No, we've noticed good examples everywhere through the years, as I'm sure you have—or will.

For example, there was "Hannah, The Hungry Swan," our high school algebra teacher. She often stood on one foot, held the other foot behind her back, stretched her long thin neck, preened her single forehead curl, and crooned equations over her half-rims as if they were sonnets.

Also we'll never forget "Hippo the Huge" who delivered hot doughnuts to our dorm after hours when we were in college. One time we got up a collection and got Hip to go down the wet slide in nothing but his shorts. Hip was Hip—all over.

These were just a couple of the more colorful and memorable people in our past. Most of the plain ones we've forgotten.

However I've branched completely away from the Logan's Chapel Church Choir where this all began. This gift first came upon us at a young, fidgety age as we sat with our parents Sunday after Sunday down near the

front of the Logan's Chapel Church trying our best to at
least appear worshipful.

Appearing worshipful requires one to be quiet, serious,
and to look straight ahead. In most church configurations,
looking straight ahead results in one looking straight into
the faces of the choir members. Looking straight ahead at
the Logan's Chapel Church Choir for a full hour produced
a *conversion* experience for Len and me.

It happened just this way. To fight off the fidgets and
the resulting pinch from Mother, one of us—Len, I think—
was inspired with this edifying diversion. Not a game,
mind you, this was to be educational, a primitive do-it-
yourself zoology.

Study would begin with one of us searching the faces of
the choir members, receiving a vision and then quietly
writing the name of an animal on his bulletin. The other
player/worshiper would then select the matching choir
member.

Matching was not difficult—not nearly as difficult as
maintaining the worshipful appearance when you scored.
Trying to muffle and mask the joyful outburst resulting
from finding a perfect match sometimes led to a low moan-
ing sound that impressed the charismatics in the congre-
gation but made Mother very suspicious.

Discovery of this mind-expanding activity improved our
enthusiasm for church. We looked forward to going each
Sunday to take stock, so to speak, and see what new creatures may have joined the choir. Mother never guessed
why we got so much more interested in church than
before.

Believe me, the Logan's Chapel Church Choir was overstocked with choice subjects. All the choir members at Logan's Chapel looked special if one had the proper interest in them and studied them. I can't remember there being a single ordinary-looking human being in that choir.

I can still picture those choir members today, just as they sat Sunday after Sunday. Among the sopranos, there was May Belle Brown, "The Lizard." We didn't know the word chameleon yet. Anyway it wasn't her color changing that was all that good. It was her quick head turns and darting eyes. And it was that little flap of skin that hung down and swung wildly trying to keep up with May Belle's chin, just like a lizard.

Most of the other sopranos were birds of some sort. One especially comes to mind. Honestly I don't remember her real name—Roper, I think. "Mrs. Leghorn" was the way I always thought of her. Imbedded in my mind is her likeness to many of our White Leghorn laying hens: the sloped eyes, the pursed lips, and the curious way she tilted her head from side to side. Mrs. Leghorn dressed a lot in white and often wore a soft red hat that flopped over and became her comb. One day at school I slipped and called her son "Bobby Leghorn," but he didn't get it.

The bass section was the most fertile section of the choir. Besides "Catfish Simpkins," there was "Armadillo Dollarhide" and Judge "Bull Malloch." Judge Malloch wasn't a Judge at all. Judge was his name. (He had a brother named Senator and a sister called Easy, but that's another story.)

Judge Bull Malloch was not a judge, but he was a bull. Everyone recognized that, not just because of his bulk and deep voice, but the way he snorted and stomped when he walked. Also he bellowed well on the rare occasions they gave him a solo part in church.

The tenor section was mostly exotics, not just animals we knew around Columbia county. There was Claude, "The Camel," Sumner. With those legs and that hump Claude looked the part but didn't live up to it well. I guarantee he couldn't go a week without a drink and barely through church.

Fred Farmer we called "Felix the Cat." He looked and acted exactly like an impish cartoon character of that day. I hated to make eye contact with Felix, for I was sure he was in on what we were doing.

"Snake Simpson" not only looked like a snake but according to Dad had a forked tongue. Snake was good on the high notes and great on scales.

The full-figured Beene sisters dominated the alto section. We innocently labelled them "The Canadian Honkers." It was much later—about puberty—that we understood the full thrust of it, but the name fit and it stuck.

We hadn't had enough schooling to know all God's creatures, so not every alto got immediately classified. For example, there was good old Mrs. Canfield. She had a memorable one-of-a-kind face, but we couldn't match it to any animal we knew. She had big doleful eyes and slowly chewed her gum with a slight cross bite. Years later in our World Geography class on Peru, the teacher put up a big head-shot poster of a llama. In loud unison Len and I chorused out, "Mrs. Canfield." The teacher shook her head over our explanation but finally let us come back to class. I guess she didn't know Mrs. Canfield.

It's up to you whether you'll want to try this with your church choir. If you do, your preacher is probably going to wonder what you've been up to or what you think he's been up to.

I don't advocate or defend this practice. Like all snobbery, it finally comes home to roost. You are probably on someone's list yourself. I know Len and I are.

After college when our faces and bottoms began to fleshen up, our young nephews joked a lot around us about "The Walrus Twins." We knew who they meant. At least they've never forgotten us.

And recently my visiting grandson said, "Daddy Ben, every time I look at you right in the face, it makes me miss Beau." Beau is his St. Bernard, but the match didn't offend me. He loves and trusts Beau more than nearly anyone and will never forget him.

I'll settle for that.

Sailing, Ballooning, and Other Forms of Homemade Fun

Sometimes my own children annoy me by complaining, "Daddy, I don't have anything to do." Well, shoot! There's a bunch of things they haven't tried yet. I tell my kids about some of the things Len and I played when we were growing up, and they just look at me like I am crazy.

Most times my kids won't even try the things we had so much fun doing. For example, Len and I spent many a fun Saturday afternoon down in the pasture sailing bucket lids. My children won't try that. Even on those rare occasions when they can find a bucket lid, they just refuse to try it.

We didn't need bought games or someone to teach us a game. Len and I were innovative. We made up a lot of fun things to do.

I remember one time we went to town with my Daddy. We saw some kids with balloons. We liked those balloons and wanted one. We didn't have any money to buy a balloon, but that didn't stop us. We said, "Shoot, we can make a balloon. All we need is something we can inflate with air." When we got home, we wasted half a day trying to blow up a tow sack. Not a really bad idea, just poor raw material.

It was much later—hog killing time—before we discovered a pig's bladder. We told the neighbor boy it was a balloon and got him to blow the bladder up. It made a fair balloon and even better football. That may catch on.

Another thing Len and I used to do for fun was to fish. We were born wanting to fish. Even as little ole bitty boys, we wanted to go fishing, but we never had been fishing. We lived forty miles from any water. (We had heard it took water.)

We talked about fishing, dreamed about fishing, and made up stories about going fishing. We even went so far as to save up our egg money and buy some fishing tackle. Isn't that crazy? We would sit out on the back steps and make out like we were fishing.

One day we got a great idea. (I ought not to tell this. It may reflect on my sanity. However it's the gospel truth and I can't explain it—just report it.) We baited our hooks with corn and called the chickens.

Some of those old hens could really pull, too. It upset the egg schedule for a while. Mother thought the rooster had gone bad. We didn't tell her any differently until we were grown. She started to switch us even then, but we were smart enough to plead insanity. She believed us.

One other game is worth mentioning because with the election and all it may be about to make a comeback. I saw two men practicing it on television last week.

This was usually a Sunday afternoon game, particularly if we had company. To play, we would go out into the barnyard lot. When a player's time would come, he would get a pitchfork. Then he'd find a cow pie—just the right consistency. You know what I mean? If you don't know and ever get into a game, you'll learn really fast.

The object of the game was to stick the pitchfork in the cow pie and throw it up against the side of the barn. The player who could throw it the highest and make it stick the longest won. My Daddy called that game *politicking.*

We had a world of fun playing, but I sure don't want to give the impression that we played all the time. Goodness gracious no, we had chores on top of chores.

One of the jobs I had was to turn the chickens. That's turn the chickens. Every night before I went to bed I had to go out and turn the chickens because we didn't have a chicken house and the chickens roosted on the well curb. My children and others don't believe me when I tell them that and other stories about how we grew up. They usually say, "I don't believe you grew up that way. All right, how did you get into football and all. You say you played football."

Yes we did grow up that way there at Logan's Chapel. We went to school at Logan's Chapel through grade schools. But when we got old enough to go to high school, we had to start going in to "town school" we called it.

My Daddy bought us a horse and Len and I would ride this horse into town to go to high school every day. As we would leave in the afternoon, we kept noticing these boys in the field. About the third or fourth day we stopped, and the coach came over.

He said, "Hey, why don't you boys try out for the team?"

"What team?" I asked.

"The football team," he said.

"Naw, sir," I said, "I don't know anything about football."

"Ah, well," he said, "There's not that much to it." He said, "You old country boys are tough and used to work. Usually do right well at it."

He said, "It looks like your brother there has already been practicing; got those scratches around on his face."

"Naw, sir," I said, "Since we found out we were coming into town school, Len's been trying to learn to eat with a fork."

"Let me give you a tryout," the coach said. "I'll throw you the ball and you run through those boys, around the goal post, back through those boys, and back here to where I am."

"All right, sir, I'll try that," I said.

So the coach threw me the ball, I ran through the boys, around the goal post, back through the boys, and back to where he was.

"Say, that's pretty good!" he said. "Let me see you get down off your horse and try that."

Nothing to do, indeed. My kids are good kids. Some times they just don't have much imagination. That may be one of the reasons they are good kids.

A Man's Best Chicken

Ask the next person you meet to tell you about their favorite chicken. Don't get your hopes up though. You may be disappointed with the response you get. My experience has been that other than strange looks and a few weird recipes you won't get much return from that question.

Nearly all adults remember their childhood pets with fondness and admiration—dogs, cats, even hamsters and fish. Len and I sure do remember ours.

There were Fred, Champ, BoBo, et al. (dogs), a good old grouchy cat named Lindberg, and a special horsefly named Rover. We have a favorite story or two about each of them—stories of intelligence, courage, and loyalty. You know the type—old, sentimental, camp fire stuff. However you hardly ever hear grown ups, or even children, talk about their favorite chicken. Chicken memories just don't seem to endure with people. Not so with Len and me.

We remember a flock of great chickens. For example, we were the proud owners of Curls, the "Dominecker" chicken who got a permanent wave and crossed eyes when lightening struck near the chicken yard as he or she was getting a drink of water. Curls' gender was a mystery, but it didn't seem to matter to anyone, least of all to him or her.

The curly feathers were a sight to behold. The crossed

eyes were harder to appreciate or even to verify. You may have noticed that it's extremely hard to get a look at both of a chicken's eyes at one time.

Sadly, Curls died a premature death. Not from the lightening or other injuries, but dehydration. We never could get him or her to take another drink of water after the fateful day, just dried up. Curls left fond memories and a fine, curly, one-of-a-kind feather duster. Mother would only use it in the parlor—and we didn't even have a parlor. What a tribute. What a chicken.

One year our whole chicken flock missed being famous by just a quirk of fate. Our county agent Colonel Calvin Coolidge Sanders had talked my dad into letting him try a bold, new forced-feeding and rapid fattening experiment on our chickens. "A pot for every chicken," he called it. Before he could get started, he was transferred to Kentucky, I think and never seen or heard from again.

Our 4-H leader used to crow a lot about the three contributions chickens make to farm life. The Three F's, she called them: Food, Feathers, and Fertilizer.

Len and I added a fourth F—Flying. Len and I were always fascinated by flying—flying machines, people and things, including chickens.

Some of our fondest and most dramatic memories were of times spent flying chickens. Many was the time when other youngsters were riding horses, hunting rabbits, or smoking vines, but Len or I would say, "Let's go fly some chickens." And we would.

Some chickens fly a lot better than others. White giants are the worst. Though they appear to have all the equipment—wings, flaps, and a "humongous" rudder—they just aren't good at flying. Their weight seems always to be headed in the wrong direction.

Rhode Island Reds are not much better and have a bad attitude. If you know anything at all about flying, you know a bad attitude will lead you to a lot of trouble, cause you to fly right into the ground. A series of crashes including several of these "nose low" landings by the Reds caused a cessation of testing by orders of the Commander in Chief—Mother.

Chicken flying took off again when Daddy got the mail order Leghorns. Not only were these chickens able to fly exceptionally well, they wanted to fly. After only one or two tosses, or solos as we flyers say, these chickens began to volunteer. Some even mastered the unassisted take-off, a feat heretofore unknown to yard chickens.

They were no longer just "The Chickens." They were individuals, friends. We recognized each chicken personally, or would it be each chickenal person, calling them by name. It was the war years, so we chose mostly wartime designations.

There was Sikorsky. Not much speed or glide, but he hovered well, often spending up to half an hour hanging in one place.

And the twin-bodied P-38. Could barely fly at all but had great lines. Gained fame by winning second place in the Country Fair's Freak category. Edged out of first by a two-headed goat which could bleat in perfect two-part harmony. A real freak.

And B-17. Liked to make high level bomb runs over the clothesline on wash day. Of course he had no bombs, but he used what he had with precision. B-17 always came back.

Our best flyer and all time runway favorite was P-40. A regular flying tiger, P-40 loved to fly and it showed. He was always ready. He would lead the charge when Len and I came out into the yard. (Len kept insisting P-40 used a tiny little bugle for this. However I try to keep this stuff factual, believable, and suitable for family consumption. I heard but never saw a bugle. How would a chicken hold a bugle?)

P-40 would taxi ahead of all the others, jump up on the coop and retract his landing gear—his way of volunteering for whatever mission we had in mind. P-40 was always eager to be tossed into the wild blue yonder where he would sometimes sail and soar and swoop for an hour.

During one of these flights, P-40 distinguished himself in Chikendom for all time. He assured his place in the Chicken House of Fame along with such other luminaries as Chicken Little, Big Bird, Henny Penny, and Stan Diego.

On this great day P-40 engaged the local chicken hawk in a dog flight at three hundred feet and prevailed. After only a few minutes of warfare, the startled chicken hawk, unaccustomed to being challenged by anything in his own element—much less a chicken—tucked his plucked tail and retreated to new territory never again to return to Burton field. P-40 taxied in to a hero's welcome. The flapping was long and stirring, if not deafening.

In lieu of the Congressional Chicken of Honor which could sometimes take months to process (chickens hate processing)—months we knew P-40 may not have—Len and I decided to do the next best thing. With model airplane paint (we called it dope in those days, but we didn't know what we were talking about), we painted our top commendation in big blue letters on P-40's wings. P-40 was so proud of the tribute. He would stand on the coop and spread his wings fully and display: ARMY AIR CORPS.

Only a few weeks later, as we began to assemble for Sunday dinner (which we ate at noon in those days), I saw finery coming out that we saw only on high holidays and other special occasions:

- The John Deere sugar bowl Aunt Doll Johnson sent us from the Chicago World's Fair.
- And my older brother's autographed picture of the late, great Jimmie Rogers. Another clue to the Red Letter nature of this day was that Len and I were pressed through a refresher course in manners.

Someone mentioned that the preacher and his wife were joining us. Then it all started to come into focus. This indeed was a special occasion. Special occasions meant finery and manners and fried ch————!!

Len and I excused ourselves—which wasn't necessary since, as youngsters, we wouldn't be eating until the second table anyway—and raced out toward the chicken house barely in time to hear the fading strains of a tiny bugle sounding taps. Most of the flock was there, but it was an aimless, leaderless group. An air of chicken grief prevailed.

Just as we feared, P-40 was nowhere to be seen—gone on his last big mission, his last true measure of devotion.

P-40—now there was a real chicken.

When dinner was finally called, we didn't have to fib about it. We truly weren't hungry.

The Wrong Brothers: Another Theory of Flight

Probably you know by heart the story of the two famous pioneers of heavier than air flight. You should. They have received much good publicity. Not nearly as well known, up to now, are two other brothers—twin Arkansas farm boys—who also did some original work in the flying field.

As far as we know, Len and I were the first and only ones in Arkansas doing any serious experimental work in flying, of the kind we did. In all the years since, no one else has come forward to claim any of the credit. Yes, we had our doubters. Believe us, it's lonely to be pioneers.

Len is due most of the credit for our experiments in flying. I have tried hard to give Len all the credit. Len was the Orville *and* the Wilbur of our flying team. I was the Step-'N-Fetch-It and in one way the driving force as you will see or hear.

Len always knew he could fly. He tried to fly many times and crashed often before saner members of the family finally convinced him that to fly he needed an airplane. "Len, you need help," is an admonition Len has ignored all his life.

A lot of kids have stick horses. Len and I were among the first—and last—to "fly" stick airplanes.

We had never seen an airplane on the ground, but we had seen a few planes fly over our farm. Using close observation (from three thousand feet), primitive scientific methods, and our version of native intelligence, we were able to figure out how they did it.

We reasoned a plane's shape had a lot to do with its ability to fly. Airplane Shape: A long body with a longer wing across it and a much smaller wing across the back. Shape and a loud noise—that's about it—and a place to ride.

Based on those deductions and extensive drawing and calculations done on a Box Holder envelope from the burial association (I hope we saved this for the archives), Len made an airplane that would fly us to Shreveport. Yes, like those other pioneers, we had a challenging destination. Shreveport was ninety miles away.

History doesn't tell us, but from Kitty Hawk the Wrights were probably trying to fly to Charlotte—or back to Ohio. The Burtons were bound for Shreveport and the Louisiana State Fair.

Len's plane (I signed a release for my part in exchange for a Bob Uecker baseball card) consisted of one long two-by-four with another long two-by-four across it for the wing and a shorter two-by-four across the back. He straddled his stick airplane and told me to get in—on, actually—if I wanted to go to Shreveport.

Only to avoid discouraging Len, I decided to participate. Also it meant a free trip to Shreveport. Shreveport was to us in south Arkansas what New York City was to the rest of the country, big fair and all.

Len checked me for weapons, and I got on *board*. The term "on board" is used to this day around airports. Few know the origin. The next time you hear it, you will have a better understanding of what it means. When you get your boarding pass, it won't be the Wright brothers you think about.

The trip to Shreveport would be quick. Len estimated the entire flight would last under an hour. Ole Len was right again. I'll never forget how embarrassed I was when we put on those silly goggles, straddled the airplane—the two-by-four—and went loping down through the pasture toward Shreveport.

My main job from the back seat was to provide thrust, to go "Brrrrrtn-Brrrrrtn" as loud as I could with my lips. When we didn't stay up, Orville—er Len, that is—kept yelling, "Louder, Louder!"

Remember the Wrights didn't make it to Charlotte their first flight either. In fact the Wrights flew only 120 feet farther than we did. Len said the wind was a lot better at Kitty Hawk. I'm not so sure. I revved up a pretty good "Brrrrrtn-Brrrrrtn."

While it's true that we didn't fly far that day, we did make history. You've heard it said that "A little knowledge is a dangerous thing." In that Arkansas pasture we proved, rather, that a little knowledge may be dangerous, but it is infinitely safer than total ignorance.

"Total ignorance goes clear to the bone," or something like that, and is chronic.

It's another story, but do you have any idea how many chicken feathers it takes to totally cover a strapping nine-year-old farm boy? Len does. Dreams don't die easily.

Recently I took a trip with Len on a major airline. We had an extra long take-off roll. As the heavily loaded jet raced farther and farther down the runway, I realized that Len—now full grown—was going "Brrrrrtn-Brrrrrtn" with his lips. A few seconds later I joined in. Then Len jumped up and started calling out—first to me, then to all the other passengers—"Louder, Louder!"

So much for Wright and Wrong, we made it.

Try "Brrrrrtn-Brrrrrtn" if you ever need it on your airline. Whether it works or it doesn't, you will need medical help immediately.

The Wizards of Nations Creek*

To a real scientist, certain beliefs, myths, and theories just scream out to be investigated.

"The world is flat."

"Man can't fly."

"Elvis is dead."

Statements like those just stick in the craw of the person of science. His entire system responds with skepticism. We can't rest until the theory is either proved or disproved, never just accepted but challenged and investigated. Not for financial gain or even selfless contribution must these truisms be explored. More often, for the scientist, the motive is as Hillary's: "Because they are there."

"Cats always land on their feet" cried out to Len and me just that way. We had heard grown people repeat that old saying many times. No one explained. No one challenged. No one proved or disproved it. That blind acceptance bores into the scientific mind and festers there.

"Always lands on his feet." That seemed so illogical.

* In no way do we recommend, defend, or make light of the treatment of Lindbergh or any other animal as reported here. We earnestly hope that we all, adults and children alike, are more enlightened and sensitive today than some of us were when we were children

93

Take the word *always*. Always is never always, not one other thing is always. Could a cat have the corner on always?

"I wonder if...." "I wonder why...." "How?" A lot of great science starts just that way.

Of course Len and I weren't trained scientists. Like Edison it just came natural with us. People who knew us best said we were "curious"—once again, like Edison. We worked on a wide variety of projects just like the Great One. And, like the Wizard of Menlo Park, we had our failures. (It may seem impertinent to keep drawing these parallels with the great Edison. However the comparisons are inescapable, are they not? In my best scientific mind they are. Len's also.)

One of our most heartbreaking failures came at the end of the long, long day we spent trying to throw a rubber ball and a hoop into the air at the same time so that at the apex of each throw the ball was in the exact center of the hoop.

Had we been able to do this, the hoop with the ball in the middle would have remained aloft forever above our farm—like the picture in our sister's school book. It was much later that I learned the picture in my sister's book was of Saturn with its rings. However the ball in the hoop theory has never to my knowledge been competently disproved. Has it to your knowledge? Len and I plan to work some more on it this summer—at a lower orbit. Care to join us?

Back to a more pressing experiment—the proper scientific investigation of the highly-suspect claim that cats *always* land on their feet. There's that word again. There's something about that word always that just grates on a scientist. Oh, the price of enlightenment.

Len and I set out to give this theory a proper scientific challenge. We would let the cats fall where they would, to use a little laboratory humor. No offense, I hope.

If you know anything at all about science, you know science requires a systematic approach. Oh, we had done some random cat tossing, and the old theory seemed to hold up. We never felt it necessary to get into the heavy stuff, things like the cat juggling we had heard about from our cousin who had once visited some of the dins of iniquity in Mexico.

What we needed was a plan—a series of tests to find out once and for all if cats did indeed always land on their feet. Our minds were more than open, and then some. We surely did not want to be or intend to be cruel, but obviously we needed the help of a cat. Fortunately we had Lindbergh, a long time but generally non-participating member of the family. He was the real hero of this story.

Lindbergh was not particularly cooperative, but he was easy to catch and was forgiving—or had a short memory. And he only left home at night. All this was good because the experiments were to last several days. We decided that three experiments would validate or invalidate the widely held belief about a cat's sense of balance.

The experiments were to be planned and conducted in an orderly manner. All results were to be observed and recorded until we reached a "provable and replicable conclusion." (Len copied that part out of a book.) We were determined not to fail.

Len said Edison failed more than three thousand times

trying to invent the light bulb, and we sure didn't want to be like Edison. What leadership!

The story is best told in our own records, that is from our lab notes (actually the barn but who would ever put any faith in barn notes?):

Experiment Number 1

Hypothesis: The cat's secret lies in his good eyesight and ability to locate the ground from any posture.

Test: Blindfold the subject, turn him on his back, and drop from a high place.

Results: Failure. Lindbergh unruly and uncooperative after two hours of attempting to blindfold. Apparently fails to understand his potential place in history.

Ancillary findings: Cats have practically no forehead.

Experiment Number 2

Hypothesis: The cat's uncanny balance is a product of his acute hearing.

Test: Stuff cotton into the cat's ears until he sits perfectly still even when the dog barks. Toss into the air and observe landing. ·

Results: Incomplete and inconclusive. Cats are sensitive about ears. Lindbergh unusually violent. Scratched friendly lab assistant (me). Removed cotton as fast as inserted. Idea to restrain subject's hands and feet abandoned as impractical. It would make heart of the experiment—the landing—awkward and meaningless.

For Sale: Two pairs of paw cuffs. Barely used.

Experiment Number 3

Hypothesis: The cat's ability to land on his feet results from his intelligence and/or rapid processing of visual and oral data.

Test: Get the cat drunk and drop from a high place. Two methods of getting Lindbergh drunk considered. (1) Fermented pokeberry juice. Little data available on amount of pokeberry juice needed. Learned from Charles Allbright, *The Arkansas Traveler*, and verified on our own mule, that it takes ten gallons to make a zebra out of a white mule. No help here. (2) Spin the cat around until he's drunk. We had learned in a yard game that running around in several tight circles with forehead resting on a hoe handle could make one lose all one's sense of balance and direction. No luck at all in getting Lindbergh to run around hoe handle even after we cut one down to his size: 4 1/8", short oval. Then just as we began to despair, the break came. So much of good science is accidental, like penicillin, gravity, barbecue, etc.

Suddenly one of us remembered that we once got drunk spinning around on the bag swing. From there it was a short distance for two young wizards to design and make a harness for Lindbergh and swing him from the hay lift in the barn and spin him around until he was good and drunk.

Results: Victory! Just like his namesake, Lindbergh made history! On the trip down from the barn loft, Lindbergh squirmed instinctively to get his feet into the down position. In his drunken condition some error was inevitable. A miscalculation of 180 degrees was unexpected. Lindbergh came in flat on his back. Happy to report no apparent injury from the landing.

The hero did bang himself up superficially when he sprang up and sprinted full speed into the side of the barn. Just happy, I guess. Left area listing severely to port and humming "Bird in a Gilded Cage."

From those crude notes, one gets little feel for the gratification the scientist enjoys from knowing that he has contributed. No rewards, no honors, no wealth or acclaim comes close to matching the feeling one has knowing that he has unearthed the truth.

As for Lindbergh, he recovered to live many more proud years. While he was more stand-offish than ever and never spoke to Len and me again, we know he gets the same thrill we do from seeing in some of the more responsible, if unsung, journals the truth: "Cats *almost* always land on their feet." The truth makes us free!

Yesterday Is Best—with Tomorrow's Bait!

"God does not subtract from man's [please don't write and tell me God is sexist] allotted time those days spent fishing." I hope not. However I've got a feeling God gets pretty disappointed with a lot of us over fishing.

I learned some secrets about fishing a long time ago. I just wish I could always remember and practice them. God and I both would be happier. I would live longer and catch more fish, too.

Fishing is like a lot of things—sometimes good and sometimes not. We choose which it is for us—next cast, next trip, next season, always. It's largely up to us. That's one of my convictions.

There's a lot of convictions, claims, and beliefs about fishing—"Can't miss" kind of stuff. The fisherman is convincing because he believes what he's saying and wants to go forth and share it. You, too, will want to believe every one of these tips. And you probably will believe them, at least for a while. That's okay, as we shall see. Believe 'em really hard and as long as you can.

Fishing certainty applies to tackle, places, days, (most often, the best day was "yesterday") moon phases, depth and—the most popular item of all—*bait*. Through the years I've heard hundreds of hot tips about "the only bait to use, etc." I've tried most of these tips, with varying degrees of success. Many had cooled by the time I used them; some had gone stone cold.

Also I've kept a list of the best baits. Some, I'm willing to bet, you haven't used—yet. The list is not finished; it's alive and growing. "Disgusting, as well," my wife adds.

Just last week, my barber told us a friend of his caught twenty-one "Good uns" at Shady Lake. "You would never guess what he caught 'em on," he baited.

I wouldn't bite. I know a Catch-22 when I hear it coming. But some innocent soul asked him, "What?"

"Broiler Cheeks," was Slick's proud reply. "They were just eatin' them up. It's the only bait to use."

I knew broiler cheeks would be the only bait used for a while by everyone present. Everyone, that is, who could find out what a broiler cheek is. I figured I wasn't the only one who didn't know, but no one let on. Most of the broilers I've seen were real skinny in the face—not much cheek at all. Broiler cheeks would be another "sure fire" bait for my list.

In the public interest, I've decided to publish my incomplete list of "can't miss" fish baits. These have been collected over the years and all were guaranteed by the contributor. Incidentally some of these baits are not for the squeamish. If you catch enough fish, you won't mind a little squeam.

No artificials are included. These are the real things.
An Incomplete List of Guaranteed, "Can't Miss" Fish Baits
(Absolutely guaranteed to me by someone, some time.)

"Can't Miss" Fish Baits

> Grass hoppers, sawyers, meal worms, wax worms, earth worms, manure worms, immanure worms, cheese (853 varieties and blends), night crawlers, day crawlers, fat meat, June bugs, tumble bugs, liver (beef, pork, chicken, fish, rabbit, etc.), liver flukes, catawba worms, catlapha worms, corn, corn borers, cut bait (use your imagination), wasp, wasp larvae, *Spam, Treet,* and other imitators, rag weed pod worms, minnows, turtle parts, chops, bag worms, mountain oysters, mussels, snails, slugs, hellgrammites, feathers, grubs, toes, old undershirt.

Okay, you're right. I agree that a couple of odd ones popped up there, "toes and old undershirt"? Those do need some explanation. Don't get down on them yet though.

One day Len and I were fishing for crawdads on Grandpap's branch—fishing, not catching. Things had gone sour all day. We were both fighting a bad attitude and each other. Fat meat (it's on your list) had been such a good bait for us for so long but was just not getting the job done. We found not one crawdad, but we didn't quit. We redeployed.

The two of us sat down and dangled our bare feet in the water to rest and to think. In a moment we felt something. Crawdads!

We found that by wiggling our big toes under water we could attract the crawdads. When we felt one crawl across our foot, we would simply reach down and grab him. Believe it or not, it worked on crawdads and it may work on lobsters and shrimp too since they are kinfolks. In salt water it may require longer legs.

Try toes the next time you experience a slump in your crawdad fishing. If it doesn't work, you probably should have tried it yesterday.

The undershirt experience is a similar example—another case of a blind hog with a good attitude finding a guide dog, to improve an old adage. On this particular day, Len and I were fishing in the "big leagues." We had hiked over to Uncle Jim's pond the second day in a row to catch another big string of perch.

Fishing consecutive days is one of the better defenses for the "should have been here yesterday" rule. We had been here yesterday and it had worked. We had caught a nice bunch of big ones fishing betsy bugs (see your list). However today was a bust so far. The water was muddy from the overnight rain and nothing was biting. Len was grumpy and ready to quit and go toe dangling for crawdads. I held out hope and continued to fish.

Then it hit me. The perch so eager to bite just yesterday were still willing. They just couldn't see the dark bugs. What was needed was a lighter-colored bait, something the fish could see in the turbid water.

The only thing light colored I could find was my white undershirt—well, off-white actually. I tore off a small, narrow strip, attached it to my hook and cast it out. Whammo! A good fat keeper bit, then another and another until I had the nice string you see in the picture.

Now I've answered all the questions I care to about whether or not it helps if the undershirt has been worn several days. I won't share all my secrets. Mother did complain some about the tear in my undershirt. "Probably moths," I covered, and went right then and put moths on my list of baits.

Len kept saying fish wouldn't bite something as unlikely as an undershirt. He was right, he didn't catch a fish all day.

Maybe here's the best fishing lesson of all. There's a lot of right ways to fish and to do most everything. Our success usually has to do, not with our methods, equipment, and bait, but with what we believe in and are enthusiastic about.

The other day I ran into my neighbor Halfbright. He said he hated to go to town anymore. "Nearly everybody I run into is a stranger," he grouched. With an attitude like that, Halfbright might just as well have stayed in town. It surely wouldn't do him a bit of good to go fishing—not even yesterday.

Now, to continue that list of "can't miss" baits:

Cotton seed cake, moths, broiler cheeks, pig tails, dough balls (647 recipes for these), betsy bugs, frogs, tree frogs, lizards, spring lizards, bees, salamanders, crawfish, crayfish, midges, crawdads, crawdad tails, shrimp, pork rind, roaches, black crickets, grey crickets, sponge, stink bait (104 varieties and strengths), perch, bullheads, bacon, soap, dog food, blood, blood worms, chubs, hellbenders, salmon eggs, marshmallows, raisins, pecan worms, cotton worms, common worms, May flies, June bugs, bologna, press meat, hog head cheese, souse meat, Canadian bacon, frankfurters, prunes, hog eyes, grapes, maggots, maggits, horse flies, deer flies, dragon flies, fire flies, buttons, slicks, beads, water dogs, surgical hose, fish scraps, squid, sardines, mullet, road kill (endless varieties, ages and grades), gizzards, acorns, peach worms, paws, paw paws...and still growing.

Just a word in closing about the proliferation of the bait sub-cults. Some that are already officially organized in California are the following:

Baits in combinations
Size of the offering
Shape of the offering
Aging of bait
Various ways of holding your mouth right.

Now with computers, maybe one day soon, we'll get it all figured out. In the meantime, the fish just go right on being fish and taking little note of any of this. Fish are too busy watching out for the guy or girl who thinks today is the best day in history to be fishing, or doing anything else.

God sure won't take away a day like that from anyone.

Barnum and Burton: The Ding-A-Ling Brothers

June, 1938, I think, was the first time I said to Len, "Len, you are no Sam Walton." He agreed but didn't understand it then. I didn't either. However it seemed like the right thing to say. It makes a heap of sense today which just goes to show you, if you know what I mean.

Well, anyway, I started out to tell you about Len and me—and some of our business enterprises when we were growing up. We had a bunch of them. So many, in fact, that we had a hard time settling down on a successful one.

Daddy said we came by this naturally. "Took it after one of your uncles on your Mother's side. All his life your Uncle Alfred was a regular business *typhoon*, a real blow hard," Daddy was fond of saying.

Whatever the source, from a young age, Len and I felt driven to start a business of our own "and get rich." "Anything but this farm work," we would usually add when Daddy wasn't around.

One thing we had going for us was the fact that we both had a brother—each other. That's an advantage in business. Have you noticed that? We looked up to several successful brother teams back then: The Ringling Brothers, The Marx Brothers, The Wright Brothers. And right there in Magnolia, you had the Brothers Brothers, attorneys. "The Brothers In Law" is the way they put it on their sign.

So we had the advantage of those good examples right to begin with—and a bunch of great ideas. I admit that some of our ideas were foolish, others, down right hairbrained. They were mostly Len's, as I recall.

Barnum and Burton and the Biggest Top

I guess our most elaborate and time-consuming venture was the circus we were going to put on. Having been to a circus ourselves, we knew what to do. And we did it—for weeks and weeks and months.

First, we needed a big tent. "For the crowds," Len said. I wondered how big a tent we needed at Logan's Chapel with just the one family, counting us, living right in the area. Len would get a far-away look in his eyes and say, "If we build it, they will come." I never knew where a dream like that came from—or went.

After wasting weeks planning the tent, we decided that with the weather starting to warm up, a regular tent might get too hot. That problem didn't stop us for long. Len said that by trying really hard, we could *imagine* a tent. We would ask the paying customers to do the same thing—maybe cut the price of admission for their trouble.

So we went out in the middle of a freshly plowed field and scratched a half-acre circle on the ground and started calling it "the tent." It was amazing to me how quickly it actually became a tent. It worked better than you might think. We got no complaints, and we had plenty of room for everything—and everybody.

With the tent up providing a shady place to practice, we then needed animals and acts of various kinds. Tents, animals, and acts, that's about all there is to a circus when you think about it—and people or "suckers," as Len and Mr. Barnum called them. Len promised that they would come.

For animals, Len wanted to use all goats because we had a lot of them. I had to remind Len that everybody in Columbia County had as many goats as we did, or more. It wouldn't be safe to get up a crowd of people dumb enough to pay to see our goats. We needed animals that were different and exciting.

Like a lot of inexperienced businessmen, we probably started out too big, too many different acts. By the time we could get one act trained and perfected, another one would forget all of what we had taught. Or, as was the case with our zebra, they would just walk off somewhere.

Our zebra was actually our white mule we had striped with "paint" made from pokeberry juice. He didn't know the first thing about performing or about loyalty either. Not only that, we had to chase him down and repaint him after every little shower. Who needs a zebra?

Some of the other animals were about as uncooperative. Len wasted several weeks trying to teach our young horse, Half-Paint, to walk on his hind legs with his front feet on tom walkers and be a giraffe. Half-Paint (his mother was Paint) never learned to stay up more than thirty seconds and never got over a wild, non-giraffe-like look of panic when he was up there. Finally I had to tell Len to give it up. We never would have sold any tickets to see a small, grey, short-necked giraffe anyway. Even goats would have drawn better.

We lost our feature act when Fred, our usually-obedient, old, full-blooded, part-bulldog got surly and tore off and chewed up the snout and big ears we had made for him. He showed no interest in being Arkansas' first pygmy elephant.

Even with a big tent and the cheerleading of "Mr. Walton," it was hard for me to keep my enthusiasm up for a one-ring circus with no elephants. The human acts did not help matters. We got no cooperation from our two teenage cousins J. C. and the other J. C. we called James Cleveland for long. We were working with them to appear as giant midgets from Madagascar. They could not, or would not, learn the few jungle-like phrases we wanted them to repeat and went off mumbling "just like their Uncle Alfred."

Our circus still has not opened, but we haven't completely given up. We talk about it from time to time—picture the crowds and the money. And the tent is still out there right where we drew it and, except for a few weeds, as good as ever.

Mainly we just got busy with other more promising enterprises like the paper route.

Wanna Buy A Grit? Anyone? Anything?

The ad I ripped out of a magazine probably said a lot of other things in the fine print. However I only saw the part about "your own free route bag" and "winning a bicycle." The small coupon was really easy to fill out. We got it filled out and signed and in the mail that very day, to Chicago I think. The next day, we met the mail carrier but Mr. Dendy said things took longer than one day to come back from Chicago. We met him every day anyway for about ten days awaiting our next bonanza. Mr. Dendy was about as proud as we were when the nice, fat brown package finally arrived. We ripped it open to find the big white cloth bag with the wide shoulder strap and GRIT printed across it in beautiful red letters.

There were twenty-five neat little newspapers, all just alike. They had the word GRIT printed on them also. The price was five cents each. It was a good little newspaper with a lot of interesting news in it. Even ten days out of Chicago, it was all news to us.

The bicycle, I reckoned, would come later.

Also in the package were a letter and an important looking form with a lot of words on it. I did not understand all it said, but I noticed that the word *remit* was used a lot. Mother read the form to us and explained the deal we had entered. We were to sell the twenty-five papers for five cents each and remit the money to the company. Then the company would send us more papers; we would remit and so on. Then one day they would send us the bicycle.

Easy enough. Let's sell papers!

Mother bought the first GRIT. She gave us a beautiful, cool nickel and said she would buy one every week. Hot dawg! Now we're in business. Now we will get rich—and a bicycle, too!

Mother, our best customer, also told us that Aunt Mattie had said she would buy one. Aunt Mattie lived in the Welcome community, clear across the county, so we had to mail hers. That cost us six cents postage, but Len said a customer is a customer and we would make it up in volume. I humored him, so he put me in charge of volume.

Now then, who else? Uncle Jim and Aunt Ola were our nearest neighbors—only a mile away. "Uh oh, they read only the Bible." "Who else, Mr Walton?" That bicycle would sure come in handy now.

Three weeks later, with twenty-three aging GRITs on hand, a cash flow of ten cents, and a second letter from Chicago which again contained the word *remit* a lot, this time in bold print, we began to feel desperation. New GRITs are hard enough to sell, old ones almost impossible. Our fantasies ran to things like the "long arm of the law" and hearing our own story on Gang Busters. Phrases like the slammer, Big Al, and "you dirty rat," crowded our minds and were even more ominous than before.

We were scared and discouraged. However we did not just surrender. We fought hard for our bicycle and our freedom. Len swiped my sister's megaphone to help us with a last ditch, door-to-door campaign, but it didn't help, with no customers—not even any doors—in the pasture and the woods. We argued about a "buy one, get one free" sale and what Len wanted to call a "Blue Light Special." Nothing worked.

Finally Mother set us down and talked to us long and seriously about things like "contracts, responsibility, and word-as-bond." She then declared our bankruptcy. She asked for the ten cents in the company treasury and said she would put $1.15 with it and remit it to Chicago.

"And, young man," she said to each of us. (When she

addressed us as "young man," it wasn't a commentary on our age or stage of development. It was her version of, "Will the defendant rise." We knew there would be no plea bargains, probation, or community service but a lot of court costs.) "As for the twenty-three copies of GRIT we just bought," she went on, "we must not waste them. I want you to read them up. I want each of you to begin now and read every word in each one of them." And we did.

Although the penalty took us several days, it was a fair and reasonable punishment and a valuable lesson. (So much kinder than Big Al would have been to us.) I can still quote some of the passages from GRIT, August 12, 1939. The answers sure help me in trivia games. Problem is, those questions are not raised much anymore.

The most unpleasant thought in all this is that there is probably an old "new" bicycle rusting away in a warehouse somewhere in Chicago with our names on it.

Those are only two of the many tries Len and I made to find our own skin game and become rich. They were not even the worst flops.

For example, there was the Model Airplane Shop we opened in the storm cellar. In six months of operation, we never had one customer, other than each other. Even Mother and Aunt Mattie were able to resist those bargains.

And there was the muscadine juice stand we set up out in front of the house to refresh thirsty passers-by, if any. There weren't any. Not a single person passed by the stand in the three weeks muscadines were ripe. But as the ever-optimistic "Mr. Walton" said, "We didn't miss a sale and we were able to move all the inventory." What a guy!

The common thread in all our business failures seems to have been a lack of customers. Even today, I notice a lot of businesses failing for that reason.

Striking it Rich

No, Len and I never had much success in business—then or later. However we did get rich. We have our health, our original wives (one each), hundreds of memories like these I've shared, and between us a beautiful group of twelve happy and healthy children and grandchildren (and still counting) who think we are special—and funny.

That's what I call rich.

FODDER

"Did You Say Relish Spread?"

(The Beginning of my Fifty-Year Fear of Kroger Stores)

You'd of thought we were starving. We weren't starving, not even hungry. We had loads of good, home-grown, home-cooked food daily. However this cake-like food was something else. It was store bought. It was absolutely the greatest taste either of us had ever experienced.

Fay had only shared that little remaining bit, crumbs mostly. But it was enough to set Len and me wild to taste it again. "We've got to get our own soon and a lot of it!" We hadn't shown near that much energy all day.

The new mission dominated our thoughts. Standing hoe-bound in a hot Arkansas corn field, we felt that goal seemed logical and achievable and worth any sacrifice. Strange, forbidden fruit afflicts one's reasoning that way. With two's, it's more than twice as bad.

Len and I did a lot of farm work or went through the motions. That particular Saturday the motion was hoeing corn. Working or motioning was made even more difficult by the distractions we had to endure: rabbits, birds, and airplanes. The afternoon C&S to Shreveport was always good for ten, fifteen minutes of rich discussion of the

"Theory of Flight—a Corn Hoer's Perspective."

The distant view of Mother and Fay, our teen-aged sister, coming across the field from the direction of the highway was intriguing enough itself—good for several minutes of creative hoe-leaning and puzzling. As they got closer our interest turned to frenzy—feeding frenzy.

"They are eating something! They have walked to the store! Mother and Fay are eating something store-bought."

Whatever it was, we knew instinctively that it had to be exotic and larruping and scrumptious—better than anything we'd ever eaten in our lives. That's the way all store-bought food was when you never had any.

The two hoes hit the ground simultaneously. We didn't sign out, pass go, or say "May I." We took off in giant strides to investigate and to beg.

"Save me a bite, Fay," we pleaded as we ran. "What is it?" we asked, as if it mattered.

Her answer only deepened the intrigue. It was a name we'd never heard but didn't question. Our minds were on store-bought—case closed, minds closed.

When we reached them, there was only a small bit remaining—a sweet, sticky bread. After taunting us a little about how delicious it was, my sister halved the remains for us.

Aw man! We agreed that it was the most heavenly taste ever. I even went back to pick up the cellophane wrapper and lick the last traces from it. I think I can still taste it today—probably a world record in that category.

"The Plan" started forming immediately. We had to have more of this wonderful food at the earliest possible time. We hungrily mouthed what Fay had called it. The name was new and catchy, but Fay had said it earnestly and with a straight face. We knew it was correct. Our drive was to experience that taste again, and a lot more than the tiny portion we had out in the field.

Len and I held strategy sessions regularly, mainly counting our money and drooling. Counting the money went quickly. There was little available. We knew it would take a full quarter or more. After two weeks, we had only accumulated a few pennies.

Mother usually guessed what was going on, and I never knew her not to be on our side. Mother always found a way. She put our drive over the top by letting us sell a dozen eggs. "For Crayolas," I believe she said, but with her characteristic knowing wink.

Finally the day was here. "Hot dawg!" We had permission to leave school at noon and go to the store. We each checked the sweaty coins in our pockets one hundred and seventy-three times in class that morning. I'm foggy about what else went on in school.

Our plan was to leave class at noon and walk the few blocks to the big Kroger store to make the purchase. At last we were going to re-experience the cornfield high. Oh, anticipation! Oh, ecstasy! We could barely wait. Soon, we would wish we had.

The Kroger store was big by 1937 standards, and ours. They probably had in that store everything there was. Our transaction was simple and well-rehearsed. Len elected me spokesman. The vote was one to one, but he said I deserved to win. I accepted the honor.

Confidently and joyfully, I strode right up to the counter and ordered our long cherished treat.

"What did you say?" I can still clearly picture the tall, blonde Kroger manager who waited on us that day. I see the mix of amusement, pity, and disbelief on his face as he asked me to repeat my order.

Len eased back a step as he began to sense the first sickening wobble of a wheel about to run off. I asked again but with less confidence than before. The perplexed look returned to Mr. Kroger's face.

"Did you say relish spread?" he asked.

My voice and chin quivered as I made one final, hopeless grasp. "No, sir, I want *Belch Bread*," I weakly responded, hoping now for some kind of quick closure— any kind.

Len and I were country and green but not altogether inexperienced. We had stepped in it before. We were smart enough to know that we had stepped in it with both feet this time—all four, actually.

It always hurts to make a fool of one's self. It doubles the hurt to share it with your identical twin, quadruples it to also watch the collapse of an air castle you've built all by yourselves.

Much later I realized the "Food of the Gods" in the cornfield that day was a common cinnamon roll. All the rest was unbridled, run-away imagination. Fay was mortified to find out what we had done. She was sure that her classmates would find out somehow what dunces her little brothers were. She never intended to dupe us. She just misjudged our naiveté or ignorance. "Innocence," Mother always said in our defense.

Len and I were embarrassed, too. I walked many an extra block through the years to avoid going by that

Kroger store. I couldn't risk having the manager recognize me and remember. Even today, fifty years later, I cautiously glance around when in any Kroger store for fear he might be on duty.

I was grown before I gained a full appreciation for the diplomacy displayed by the Kroger man that day. He let two little twin country second-graders down as easily as he possibly could by saying earnestly and without laughing, as we backed out of his big store, "No boys, we don't have Belch Bread yet, but we will be watching for it."

"And *listening*," he might have added, but didn't.

Getting Close to
God at Dry Creek

"We had better be thoughtful when we praise or ridicule someone, particularly a child. We may be shaping a life forever and thereby the course of history."

If Lincoln, or Jesus, or Will Rogers, or one of those others we like to quote never said that, they meant to. It's one of the truest things there is. It can be the greatest power you and I ever have right in our hands.

Somewhere in cavernous War Memorial Stadium in Little Rock is a sign marking what is probably our family's high water mark when it comes to important people. Chiseled in the granite of the dedicatory plaque for that storied old stadium is the name of our first cousin Blank Blank, a member of the Commission that planned, built, and helped pay for that facility. There are many other names on that plaque, but I can't tell you a one of them, not even the Governor's. I've been by there many times to stare at Blank's name and even touch it when no one was looking.

Of course Blank is not his real name, but it will do for this purpose. He wouldn't like this attention. The interesting thing is that Blank made it there at all or made it anywhere. Like a lot of children, Blank stumbled out of the blocks trying to get life underway. Nobody's fault. It happens. Born to good, conscientious parents, he still had a hard time finding his comfort zone. A stammerer and a bed wetter, increasingly withdrawn and anti-social by age five, Blank was a looming heartbreak to his desperate parents.

Matters came to a dramatic turn for Blank at the annual extended Smith family-reunion-and-dinner-on-the-grounds held at "the old place" when Blank was going on six. Families trekked in from all over for the three day event. The groups were many and big and spanned four generations.

The fraternal bond wore thin among cousins early in the July heat and Blank had been in two fights by mid-morning of day two. So much for the relative thickness of blood and water. Then just before the huge dinner was served, it occurred that peace and quiet had broken out among the children. Someone quickly guessed why. Blank had disappeared. Gone!

Frightened and panicky, every able body joined the search. Highs, lows, barns, wells, storm cellars, cars, wagons, chicken houses, outhouses, everything was inspected. Men, women, and children were running hither and yon calling, "Blank, Blank, Blankkkkkk."

"Answer me, Blank."

"Oh, Blank!"

Finally from his rocker, the venerable old patriarch of the clan got someone's attention and said, "I'll bet he's down at Dry Creek."

Jumping at any suggestion, the swifter searchers made a dash down to the small creek in the back of the pasture, still calling, " Blank. Oh, Blank."

Once there they almost stumbled over the small, quiet lad sitting in the shadows, calmly fishing. He was unharmed except for mosquito bites. To ward off the mosquitos, he had covered his face with mud making himself almost invisible.

"Didn't you hear us calling, Blank? Why didn't you answer?"

"Yeah, I heard you," he admitted, "I was enjoying listening. First I knew you all cared."

Returning to the house and dinner, one of the grateful searchers asked Papa Smith how he knew Blank was down at the creek.

"Well," he said, "Yesterday I took Blank fishing down there. He caught several good fish and had a good time doing it. Coming home I told him I had seen a lot of fishermen in my time, but I thought he was the best young fisherman I had ever seen.

"Why, that boy lit up all over, got two inches taller on the spot and you know what he told me? He said, 'Papa, fishin' is what I'm gonna do for the rest of my life!' "

We didn't hear much about Blank's problems after that, but we heard a lot about his deeds. He fished often and caught lots of fish and became better and better at it. He got along a lot better with everyone. School was a breeze.

Then as Blank got older, he went all over the country fishing. There were trophies, pictures in the paper and all to prove it. People called for his advice and he gave it. When you thought of Blank, you thought fishing—and vice–versa.

He went to college and became a big successful lawyer—and got rich. Also he married a beautiful lady and had a fine family.

And he fought a war, although he was old enough to have legally stayed at home. In the Battle of the Bulge in 1944-45, Blank became a genuine American hero. He got metals of all kinds and was praised for his leadership and valor. He got badly wounded too but made it back home, quietly.

Being younger, Len and I looked up with pride and admiration to our hero cousin Blank. We kept clippings on him and sent him cards while he was overseas. We went to his office a few times to look at him, to see his big cars and his medals, maybe even his scars if he'd let us, and to hear some war stories and travel stories and lawyer stories, if he wished.

None of that worked.

It just beat all but every time we visited him all Blank ever wanted to talk about was fishing. You would think fishing was the most significant thing that ever happened to him.

Blank Blank, a great American. I'm mighty proud he's our cousin. Papa Smith sure knew what he was doing that day at Dry Creek. I hope I do, and you do, when the next chance like that comes along for us. It's as close to *being* God as we're ever apt to get.

FROM HERE TO MCNEIL

From Here to McNeil, and Beyond

Recently I was telling Len about stopping at a driving range and hitting a few golf balls. Naturally I wished to impress him with how far I was hitting the ball these days. I knew he would expect me to exaggerate my best shot, and I intended to meet his expectations.

My description surprised me as much as it did Len. Leaping spontaneously from the deep, forgotten folds of my grey matter came the ultimate answer to every "how far" question raised during our childhood: "I hit one golf ball from here to McNeil!"

That flagrant but familiar overstatement stunned us both into boyish giggles and reminiscences. How many hundreds of times had we used that phrase growing up?

"I threw a rock from here to McNeil."

"I bet that kite string reaches from here to McNeil."

"You can hear Mother's whistle from here to McNeil."

"That horse is gonna kick you from here to McNeil."

How Len and I savor the flash-backs triggered by that dusty old expression which I guess we originated. Who else?

"From here to McNeil" defined the unreachable, the limits of our Logan's Chapel sphere. The tiny village of McNeil was beyond our horizon—only eleven graveled miles away, just seven the way the rock flies.

"Not as far as it use to be," was Len's segue back to my golf shot. The McNeil comparison reminded us both of just how tiny our world was in the mid-thirties. Not as far, indeed, nor as fast. Our mode of travel to the outside world was a wagon, mule drawn. And what a special day when we got to ride the wagon the four miles into Magnolia, our county seat, about a third the distance to McNeil but an all day round trip.

Daddy hitched up the mules for the trip to town about once a month. Mules were ordinarily as dependable as could be; they were slow, steady, strong, and gentle. However mules do balk, though only once in a long while. But when a mule balks, he does it so well that one tends to remember it.

The term "mule-headed" was experienced I'm sure, not just made up. Someone experienced a balk and his language failed him. Characterizations like "hard-headed," "stubborn," "obstinate," not even "obdurate" properly describe a balk.

"Mule-headed!" That's what Daddy said Ole Tom was when he balked before crossing Grandpap's branch one Saturday morning when we started to town in the wagon. Tom suddenly planted all four feet at the edge of the water, put his head down with eyes wild, and hunkered down for the duration. Tom defined duration as "when he got ready."

Jacob, the other mule, wanted to go to town, the wagon wanted to go, we wanted to go, but Tom made the call.

And he made it stick. No yelling, no whipping, no pulling or pushing gained any ground. Cussing may have helped some, but it didn't move the mule or wagon an inch.

After trying it all, Daddy, who knew mules and mule-headedness, unharnessed the team and abandoned the trip. We just left Tom standing there braced for the duration. We showed him.

With a long time to plan his summary of the situation, Len said as he finally climbed down from the empty wagon, "Dad, I wish you would get horses. At least they are human." Ab didn't think Len was funny, but they could have heard me laughing from here to McNeil.

Some time during this period of our history, we began having the privilege of mixing in a few car rides with the wagon rides. These big events were the well-spaced occasions when one of our aunts or uncles visited us and offered us a ride in their car.

People aren't thoughtful that way anymore. How long has it been since someone visited you and asked if you would like to go for a ride in the car?

Len and I always accepted. We loved riding in a car with our hand out the window catching a big, firm handful of cool air. You come up empty trying that on a wagon.

We would count the telephone poles between Magnolia and Waldo as they blurred by. I got three hundred and fifty-two. Len got four hundred and eleven. If you know the right answer, let us know. We've got a bet on it.

It was during one of these car rides that I caught the first whiff of the good life—the first inkling that there just might be something good beyond McNeil.

The first car trip we ever took—a trip, not just a ride,

with clean underwear, goodbyes and all—was when our Aunt Marie took us home with her to Pine Bluff. This place was even farther than McNeil. We would never have been able to throw a rock to Pine Bluff, not even Travis Jackson, I bet, or Schoolboy Rowe could have.

Pine Bluff was also a big town. Some said thousands or more people lived there, so many that Aunt Marie didn't even know them all. It was on this trip to Pine Bluff that we saw our first two story house. Len spotted it first. I thought he described it well, but our aunt just about broke up over it. Len said, "Look, Ben. There's a house on top of a house."

Len and I saw many other things we had never seen before, like a telephone. Len saw a man in a store talking on a telephone and said, "Look, yawl, there's a man sucking a black bottle." I wanted to reach out and touch someone.

Aunt Marie had a telephone right there in her home. Len couldn't keep his hands off of it. He got it in his mind to call Mother at home and tell her about the telephone. Of course Mother would have to go all the way to the bus station in town to take the call after the bus people sent her a card and told her about it. We would have been home by then.

Once Len picked up Aunt Marie's phone and the operator said, "Number, please?" Len wasn't ready for that, so he said what he usually said when he needed more time to think. He said, "Ma'am?"

Again, the operator said, "Number please?"

Len said, "There's just the two of us here now; however, my Aunt Marie will be back in a few minutes." The line went dead and it was a good thing.

Len is right though. It's not as far to McNeil as it used to be—Pine Bluff either or Moscow. We enjoyed reliving those feelings of breaking away, of pushing our boundaries back with the help of good people like Aunt Marie, our older brothers and sisters, and others.

But you know something that bothers me, gives me a smothering spell, as my good Mother used to say? It is to think that, even today, there are little children growing up out there with a McNeil horizon, with parents unable or unwilling to help them understand how limiting it is to stop all your dreams at McNeil—and no Aunt to take them to Pine Bluff.

Even sadder in some respects is the thought that there are grown people out there that haven't yet seen beyond the horizon right over there at McNeil. Last summer I uncovered a man like that right under my nose.

I saw in myself someone who has seen (with the love and help of others) far beyond McNeil, to Pine Bluff and even Seattle, yet someone who still had one foot firmly planted back there in a little province seven miles southwest of McNeil, Arkansas and didn't realize it.

As a professional speaker, I am privileged to go all over the country to speak, sometimes even two presentations in one day. This was an occasion like that.

I was to fly into Los Angeles the afternoon before, rent a car, drive across a section of that sprawling city to a suburb where I had a program the next morning, spend the night, return to the airport at noon the next day for a short flight to my second presentation that afternoon.

The idea of driving twice across part of Los Angeles

frightened me. I dreaded it—like going into the land of the Philistines. I knew how "all those people in Los Angeles are." I had always thrown them all into that non-thinking basket. That was before I encountered the Los Angeles people I came to call *The Good Shepherds.*

There is a world of good people out there. This was a car load of them in Los Angeles.

Through a series of freak circumstances, I was running late returning to board my plane out of LAX for my afternoon program. Although I had made it all right the previous afternoon, Los Angeles was now proving to be as bad as I knew it would be; that is, as big and threatening as a country boy's imagination and a McNeil Horizon can make it.

There was an audience—to say nothing of a reputation and a speaking fee—waiting for me in a Bakersfield suburb. I was tense, pessimistic, and annoyed with this dilemma which was once a sensible travel plan. Now "scared" could be added to my list of anxieties.

When things fell apart, timing-wise, at my morning presentation, I knew I had only a slim chance to make my plane to Bakersfield. After putting a substitute speaker in the Bakersfield area on alert, I grabbed a map and plotted a "back door" approach to the Los Angeles Airport which would give me an outside chance to make my departing flight. The only problem was that this substitute route would take me right through the dark Los Angeles "jungle" I knew awaited me. I had to chance it.

Every detail would have to work perfectly. Every one did, up to a point. Suddenly my route was blocked by major construction—no detours, no signs. Blocked! I wheeled the rental car around to seek another way—sweating cups full and feeling the sickening knot in my abdomen brought on by hurry and the looming reality of being a "no show" speaker. Now add the realization that I was practically helpless in evil LA.

Getting no visual clues, I dead-reckoned a substitute course toward the massive airport. Quickly I found myself clogged up in a residential section of south Los Angeles—no thoroughfares to anywhere. I felt beaten.

Frantically, and with fearful misgivings, I pulled beside a car in the inside lane signalling a left turn. It was a big, older car with an even older driver. The car was filled to the seams with child forms behind what appeared to be a dozen sets of big brown eyes.

"A grandmother driving her grand-brood to the pool or the movie, or just avoiding the apartment heat," I reasoned. I rolled my window down and motioned that I wished to talk. I read the grandmother's lips as she said, "See what he wants, boy."

"Can you tell me the fastest way possible to get to LAX?" I appealed.

She read my urgency immediately and replied, "You got to get to the San... Naw," she decided better, "Come on! Follow me." She jerked her car over in front of mine and scratched out for somewhere. Door-to-door children were motioning me to follow their car and to speed up.

This group of cheering saints led me on a speeding, swerving, squealing, circuitous route through dozens and dozens of blocks of sweltering urban ugliness. Finally when I was within five minutes of the closing of the last window on any chance of making my flight, the grandmother slowed and pulled left. A tangle of little arms popped out from all over, motioning me by and gleefully pointing to the airport just ahead.

I passed along side with only enough time to say, "Bless your heart, I'll thank you forever."

The grandmother's response, spoken with more soul and person-to-person kindness than I've ever heard from anyone, branded my being forever. She coined the creed for the nineties and beyond. "We're all in this together," she smiled.

Overwhelmed I could only throw a big kiss to all my benefactors and hear the little boy riding shotgun say, "Good Luck, suh."

Tom T. Hall's great line bubbled to my lips as I sped away singing: "And God bless little children, while they're still too young to hate."

"My cup runneth over."

The lounge was empty when I arrived at the gate. My flight had boarded, but a smiling, empathetic employee appeared and squeaked me in. Three hours later in a Bakersfield suburb, I felt a new humility when I spoke of and gave a current example of "God's Love With Skin On."

When the terrible Los Angeles riots erupted last Spring, my reaction was changed. It wasn't my past non-thinking impatience with "Those Los Angeles people" any more. My tears and prayers were for grandmothers in old cars filled with loving little children—and for our *whole* country.

My horizon now reaches: "From Here to Los Angeles."

"We're all in this together."

Acres of Fish

When our speaker friend Frank Cooper tells us, "We're standing on the fish," I know he knows what he's talking about. It "harks me way back."

Uncle Jim's pond was like an ocean. Well it was a lot more like an ocean than Grandpap's branch where Len and I had done most of our previous fishing—a whale of a lot bigger, to use a slick metaphor.

We were sure the fish, too, would be a lot bigger at Uncle Jim's. We needed that. It was humiliating to have Fay, our sister, read a poem through one of the thin Silversides we brought home from the branch to brag about. Now we would show her.

Trouble was, in a really large body of water like Uncle Jim's pond, all the big fish were way out in the middle. Simple logic tells a born fisherman that. Simple was what we were best at.

In casting, our challenge became one of "getting it way out there." This had not been a problem before. If you got it way out there at Grandpap's branch you'd end up fishing on the other side, out on dry land where you might only catch a bird or a chicken.

Figuring out some way of getting our baited hook way out there dominated our creative efforts. Len wasted a lot of our time by insisting that we go around to the other side to cast. I humored him and we tried it. The middle of the pond turned out to be just as far from that side. I was pretty sure it would. (I now understand why I used to refer to Len as Tommy Smothers.)

We were determined though to figure out some way of getting our bait out to where the big ones were. We experimented: the sling shot idea was dangerous and a disaster for live bait; the bow and arrow had similar results plus severe cost overruns.

Many hours and arrows later we were about ready to give up on the whole plan.

Hundreds of huge fish were teeming way out there in the middle, but we just couldn't get our hook to them. What to do, what to do?

With no new ideas forthcoming, we decided to cool it, to go swimming. We dressed quickly—undressed actually—grabbed our old inner tube and jumped in. Immediately we hit on the answer of "how to get it way out there."

More accurately, like Newton's apple, it hit on us. We would prop our pole in the tube and sail it right out to the middle where all the big ones were. What genius! It's hard to be humble at times like that. We rigged her up.

We were breathless as the quiet little craft sailed away toward the whale infested waters of "the middle." The gob of writhing earth worms trailed teasingly behind with the hook hidden inside. Any moment now! Shhhh.

Shhhhhhhhhhhhhhhhhhhhhhhhhhhhhhhhh.

Nothing happened. Not one nibble. Not one tilt. After all this time of trying we finally did get it way out there and nothing happened.

That is, nothing happened until the tube bumped into the bank and the bait fell slowly into the line of stumps we had been throwing over all day. Then, boom! The pole bent. The tube tipped and began to surge across the surface creating the pond's first wake, ever. There was a whopper on the line!

First one way and then another the fish towed the tube seeking his freedom. 'Round and 'round the pond we ran trying to guess where the fish might head next. We needed to get within reach of the pole before the giant worked free.

This merry-go-chase lasted for minutes, maybe hours. We had to solve this some way. What if our cousin Myron happened by and caught us chasing a fish? Try to explain that to a serious cousin who already thinks we are odd.

Again swimming was the answer, our best chance for capturing this behemoth. Admittedly it takes the shine off fishing to have to get in the water with a fish in order to land him. But it's not as bad as chasing a fish on dry land. And anything is better than letting him get away.

So we did. We jumped right in there with the tube, the pole, and the fish and we caught him.

He wasn't the monster we thought he was. He probably swam a pound or two off during the chase, still a nice catfish though. I would like to see Fay read a poem through that baby.

That was the day we learned that "getting it way out there" is not always the answer. I couldn't help but wonder how many bragging-size fish have died of old age while Len and I, and others, stood within an easy throw, casting over them.

There's a whole pack of lessons for life in this story:
We don't have to get it way out there.

The pasture is not always greener.

More, bigger, now—none of these is necessarily better.

Excess is rarely the answer.

Frank Cooper teaches us this and Russell Cornwell in "Acres of Diamonds" teaches us this same lesson.

If you still don't understand, you may want to talk to Len or to Tommy Smothers. Ask them to talk really slow.

After forty plus years, I recently saw Uncle Jim's pond again. You know something, it's not an ocean, not nearly an ocean or even a good size pond. In fact, I've seen larger master bedrooms. Is there a lesson here, too?

Len?

Tommy?

The Martyrdom of Andy

> **So they stoned Stephen, and as they did so, he called out, "Lord Jesus, receive my spirit." Then he fell on his knees and cried aloud, "Lord, do not hold this sin against them," and with that he died. And Saul was among those who approved of his murder.**
>
> **—ACTS 7:58-60; 8:1**

St. Augustine has said that the church owes the Apostle Paul to the prayer of Stephen. Bible scholars agree that however hard he tried, Saul/Paul could never forget the way in which Stephen died.

Andy was a sweet, amusing little guy whom everyone liked but harassed just because that was the way one treated Andy Drake. He took the kidding well. Andy always smiled back with those great big eyes which seemed to say, "Thank you, thank you, thank you," with each sweeping blink.

For us fifth-graders, Andy was our outlet; he was our whipping boy. He even seemed grateful to pay this special price for membership in our group.

"Andy Drake don't eat no cake,
And his sister don't eat no pie.
If it wasn't for the welfare dole,
All the Drakes would die."

Andy even appeared to like this sing-song parody of Jack Spratt. The rest of us really enjoyed it, bad grammar and all. I don't know why Andy had to endure this special treatment to deserve our friendship and membership in the group. It just evolved naturally—no vote or discussion.

I don't recall that it was ever mentioned in this connection that Andy's father was in prison, that his mother took in washing and men, or that Andy's ankles, elbows, and fingernails were always dirty and his old coat was way too big. We soon wore all the fun out of that. Andy never fought back.

Snobbery blossoms in the very young, I guess. It's plain now that the group attitude was that it was our right to belong to the group, but that Andy was a member by our sufferance. Despite that, we all liked Andy until that day— until that very moment.

"He's different! We don't want him, do we?"

Which one of us said it? I've wanted to blame Randolph all these years. But I can't honestly say who spoke those trigger words that brought out the savagery lying dormant but so near the surface in all of us. It doesn't matter *who*, for the fervor with which we took up the cry revealed us all.

"I didn't want to do what we did."

For years I tried to console myself with that. Then one

day I stumbled on those unwelcome but irrefutable words that convicted me forever: "The hottest corners of hell are reserved for those who, during a moment of crisis, maintain their neutrality."

The weekend was to be like others the group had enjoyed together. After school on a Friday we would meet at the home of one of the members—mine this time—for a camp-out in the nearby woods. Our respective mothers, who did most of the preparation for these "safaris," fixed an extra pack for Andy who was to join us after chores.

We quickly made camp, mothers' apron strings forgotten. With individual courage amplified by the group, we were now "men" against the jungle. The others told me that since it was my party, I should be the one to give Andy the news.

I? I, who had long believed that Andy secretly thought a little more of me than he did the others because of the puppy-like way he looked at me. I, who often felt him revealing his love and appreciation with those huge, wide-open eyes.

I can still plainly see Andy as he came toward me down the long, dark tunnel of trees which leaked only enough of the late afternoon light to kaleidoscope changing patterns on his soiled old sweat shirt. Andy was on his rusty, one-of-a-kind bike—a girl's model with sections of garden hose wired to the rims for tires. He appeared excited and happier than I had ever seen him, this frail little guy who had been an adult all his life. I knew he was savoring the acceptance by the group, this first chance to belong, to have "boy fun," to do boy things.

Andy waved to me as I stood in the camp clearing

awaiting him. I ignored his happy greeting. He vaulted off the funny old bike and trotted over toward me, full of joy and conversation. The others, concealed within the tent, were quiet, but I felt their support.

Why won't he get serious? Can't he see that I am not returning his gaiety? Can't he see by now that his babblings aren't reaching me? Then suddenly he did see. His innocent countenance opened even more, leaving him totally vulnerable. His whole demeanor said, "It's going to be very bad, isn't it, Ben? Let's have it."

Undoubtedly well-practiced in facing disappointment, he didn't even brace for the blow. Andy never fought back. Incredulously, I heard myself say, "Andy, we don't want you."

Hauntingly vivid still is the stunning quickness with which two huge tears sprang into Andy's eyes and just stayed there—vivid because of a million maddening reruns of that scene in my mind. The way Andy looked at me—frozen for an eternal moment—what was it? It wasn't hate. Was it shock? Was it disbelief? Or, was it pity—for me? Or, forgiveness?

Finally a fleet little tremor broke across Andy's lips and he turned without appeal, or even a question, to make the long, lonely trip home in the dark. As I entered the tent, someone—the last one of us to feel the full weight of the moment—started the old doggerel:

"Andy Drake don't eat no cake,
And his sister don't..."

Then it was unanimous. No vote taken, no word spoken, but we all knew. We knew that we had done something horribly, cruelly wrong. We were swept over by the delayed impact of dozens of lessons and sermons. We heard for the first time, "Inasmuch as ye do it unto the least of these...."

In that hushed, heavy moment we gained an understanding new to us but indelibly fixed in our minds. We had destroyed an individual made in the image of God with the only weapon for which he had no defense, and we had no excuse—rejection.

Andy's poor attendance in school made it difficult to tell when he actually withdrew, but one day it dawned on me that he was gone forever. I had spent too many days struggling within myself to find and to polish a proper way of telling Andy how totally, consummately ashamed and sorry I was, and am. I now know that to have hugged Andy and to have cried with him and even to have joined with him in a long silence would have been enough. It may have healed us both.

I never saw Andy Drake again. I have no idea where he went or where he is, if he is. But to say I haven't seen Andy is not entirely accurate. In the decades since that autumn day in the Arkansas woods, I have encountered thousands of Andy Drakes. My conscience places Andy's mask over the face of every disadvantaged person with whom I come in contact. Each one stares back at me with that same haunting, expectant look which became fixed in my mind that day long ago.

Dear Andy Drake, the chance you will ever see these words is quite remote, but I must try. It's much too late for this confession to purge my conscience of guilt. I neither expect it to nor want it to.

What I do pray for, my little friend of long ago, is that you might somehow learn of and be lifted by the continuing force of your sacrifice. What you suffered at my hands that day and the loving courage you showed, God has twisted, turned, and molded into a blessing. I hope this knowledge might ease the memory of that terrible day for you.

I've been no saint, Andy, nor have I done all the things I could and should have done with my life. But what I want you to know is that I have never again knowingly betrayed an Andy Drake. Nor, I pray, shall I ever.

Afterword

by Len Burton
(In the Interest of Balance)

The Butt Rebuts

Having gotten this far, you will know about me. I am "Ole Len," Ben's twin bother and, according to some, the butt of many of Ben's stories. I haven't noticed that so much, but I have noticed that Ben has an over-active case of selective memory.

Most of the stories Ben has related are those in which he is the out-right hero. Or, at least, he doesn't appear to be as backward as the other participants—notably me or some of the other domesticated animals. In the interest of balance, I wish to report a couple of actual events which may bring a slightly different viewpoint to the escapades of the now, near-famous Burton twins.

On the Cutting Edge of Science

Ben has written of our interest in science and reported on some of the experiments we conducted. This interest eventually carried us into medical research. Ben and I were the earliest practitioners of the medical technique known today as dermabrasion. Actually, I was the practitioner; Ben was the practitionee.

Our father had an emery wheel, or grindstone, in his

shop in the barn. The surface of the emery wheel was rough as they nearly always are. But I discovered that when I turned the hand crank as rapidly as I possibly could, it drove the big rough wheel fast enough to become smooth. Or it appeared to be smooth.

Feeling a breakthrough coming on, I theorized that if the surface of the wheel appeared so convincingly smooth before my eyes, it would also have to feel smooth—probably. It was worth checking out.

Quickly I moved from the theoretical to the practical. To test my theory, I would have to conduct an experiment. Desiring to maintain objectivity, I choose not to conduct the experiment on myself.

I attempted first to recruit Fred, our big, white, full-blooded part-bulldog, for the honor (white mice for the small jobs, white dogs for the big ones). However Fred exhibited a short attention span when I tried to get him to stand on his hind legs and place one of his paws on the "smooth," rapidly-spinning wheel. In fact Fred annoyed me with the coy look on his face and the way he kept taking my hands in his and trying to lead. I knew that Ben had been slipping around and dancing with him again.

My second choice was a fellow scientist—Ben. Once I explained the theory to Ben and he got a good look at how smooth the flying emery wheel had become, he eagerly agreed to participate in the experiment. At this point I felt safe in un-tieing him.

Let the test begin! I exerted all my energy, drove the wheel to the highest possible speed—the faster, the smoother, according to my calculations. At precisely the right moment I nodded "ready" to my colleague (that's scientist talk). Ben placed the index finger of his left hand on the "smoothest" part of the whirring wheel and the age of dermabrasion was born. We abraized a good portion of Ben's derm all over the shop. Fortunately Ben is fairly quick; it didn't take him more than a minute or so to complete the experiment.

By using a week's supply of coal oil and all the lamp soot and spider web we could find, we got the bleeding stopped and the finger patched and disinfected. By now his finger has almost healed. I firmly believe that given another fifty years or so... Oh, well, when you are on the cutting edge of science, there is a price to pay.

The First Dying Quail

If you are a baseball fan you undoubtedly know the term "dying quail" used to describe a ball hit just over the infielders' heads to die on the outfield grass. The trajectory of such a fly ball is much like that of a Bobwhite quail after it has been hit by a load of #8s from a hunter's gun. Hence the name.

Most of us have seen a lot of dying quails, both baseballs and shot birds. Few have seen a real dying quail. Ben has but resists acknowledging it. Instead he's got this story. Well, you'll never believe the yarn he spins about how the quail in question died. Ben and his puppy Champ were the only eye witnesses, unless you want to count the quail. But I've figured this thing out.

Ben had just gotten this new puppy, a mixed-breed he named Champ. That name turned out to be prophetic because on his first trip to the woods Champ earned the title "One Time Champion Pointer of Columbia County,

Arkansas, and the World." The late Champ holds the title to this day.

Wait! I don't mean "at one time" Champ was the Champion Pointer. The title Champ holds is for pointing just that one time and getting a quail. Ben's story unfolds like this.

Ben decided to take his new puppy Champ hunting shortly after we got him, maybe the same day. Almost immediately after entering the woods Champ came to point. To Ben's unbelieving eyes, just ahead was a single, allegedly living, Bobwhite quail backed up against a log, eyeing the rigid dog and quivering as if in a spell.

Now here's where the story gets shaky. Not having a gun but not wishing to disappoint this champion dog at the dawning of an illustrious pointing career, Ben picked up the only weapon in sight and walked over and killed the quail with a *stick*.

Understand now, this is a quail, a bird known for its quickness, its ability to run, to hide, to fly with an alarming burst of sound and feathers. Yet Ben would have us believe that in a fit of sensitivity for his new dog, he killed the quail with a stick.

There was no question about the quail. Ben and/or Champ brought it home, and we had it for supper. As I recall, Champ got the biggest portion, and rightfully so. What a dog—and only a pup! With that kind of dog, we would get big into the bird hunting business in a hurry.

Not willing to test the stick method any further I talked us into getting a gun. That way Champ wouldn't be embarrassed to go hunting with us—us with our sticks.

But Champ never pointed another bird. He retired the

Championship and went to seed. Oh, he did go to the woods occasionally with us, but he would just run along aimlessly, flushing sparrows, rabbits, and quail alike. Mostly he stayed home, ate and slept and smiled, reliving that glory day I imagine.

Ben has stuck with his quail story over the years. Other than for common sense, logic, experience, native instinct, and twenty years operating a polygraph, I have little reason to doubt him. He doesn't tell the story much anymore. You'll notice he didn't put it in his book. It's like seeing a flying saucer; it's an interesting experience but you don't want to go around telling a lot of people about it.

I have thought of Ben's quail story many times over the years, and it has burdened me. It's bothersome to not believe your twin brother, but I finally came to the plausible explanation I suggested earlier. As much as I wish it were otherwise, it is easier for me to believe that Ben and Champ happened on a Bobwhite quail at the very moment that it was experiencing natural sudden death than to believe Ben killed a quail with a stick.

It's better this way anyway. Quail hunting and baseball not withstanding, Ben and Champ must have been the first, and probably the last, to come face to face with a real "dying quail."

As to the matter of being the butt of some of Ben's stories, that may be true. If it is, I will quickly say that I would rather have made the trip as the butt than to have not made it with him at all. It has been a wonderful journey.